The Electoral College and Presidential Transitions

From Election to Inauguration
An Overview of the Process

RL32611
RL32717
RL34722
R46565
LSB10515

Congressional Research Service

This document is an anthology of reports prepared by the Congressional Research Service (CRS). CRS serves as nonpartisan shared staff to congressional committees and Members of Congress. It operates solely at the behest of and under the direction of Congress. Information in a CRS Report should not be relied upon for purposes other than public understanding of information that has been provided by CRS to Members of Congress in connection with CRS's institutional role. CRS Reports, as a work of the United States Government, are not subject to copyright protection in the United States. Any CRS Report may be reproduced and distributed in its entirety without permission from CRS. However, as a CRS Report may include copyrighted images or material from a third party, you may need to obtain the permission of the copyright holder if you wish to copy or otherwise use copyrighted material.

Contents

The Electoral College: How It Works in Contemporary Presidential Elections..1

Introduction 2
Most Recent Developments: The Electoral College and the 2016 Presidential Election 2
The Electoral and Popular Votes: Different Results.................................. 2
Faithless Electors 3
Maine Splits Its Electoral Vote 3
Unsuccessful Objection in the Joint Electoral Vote Count Session 3
Public Opinion and the Electoral College: Post-2016 Election Developments 4
Constitutional Origins.. 4
The Original Constitutional System 5
The Twelfth Amendment Repairs Flaws in the Original System...................... 6
The Electoral College Today 6
Who Are the Electors?.. 7
Nominating Elector-Candidates: Diverse State Procedures 7
How Are Electoral Votes Allocated Among the States? 8
How Are the Electors Chosen? 8
The Electors' Task: Ratifying the Voters' Choice.................................... 9
Faithless Electors: Disregarding the Voters' Choice 9
2016: Faithless Electors—Ten Attempted, Seven Successful......................... 10
General Election Ballots.. 10
The General Ticket and District Systems: How the States Award Their Electoral Votes 11
The General Ticket System 11
The District System 12
2016: The District System Produces a Divided Result in Maine 13
General Election Day 13
The Electors Convene and Vote 14
Congress Counts, Ascertains, and Declares the Vote................................ 14
Objections to State Electoral Vote Returns.. 15
2016: Attempted Objections in the Joint Session to Count Electoral Votes 15
A Tie or Failure to Win a Majority in the Electoral College: Contingent Election by
    Congress... 16
2020 Presidential Election: An Electoral College Timeline 16
Criticism and Defense of the Electoral College and Reform Proposals in Brief............ 17
Criticisms 18
Defense.. 18
Proposals for Change 18
Electoral College Reform... 18
Direct Popular Election 19
Action in Congress on Electoral College Reform, 1940s-2017 19
Action at the State Level Since 2008 20
NGO Proposal: The National Popular Vote Initiative 21

Concluding Observations. 22

Counting Electoral Votes: An Overview of Procedures at the Joint Session, Including Objections by Members of Congress. 24

Actions Leading Up to the Joint Session 25
Appointment of Electors: Election Day 25
Final State Determination of Election Contests and Controversies 25
Certification by the Governor. 26
Duplicate Certificates to Electors. 26
Meetings of Electors to Cast Votes. 26
Electors' Certifications of Votes. 26
Congressional Demand for Certificates 26
Archivist's Transmittal of Certificates to Congress 27
Date for Counting Electoral Votes 27
Providing for the Joint Session 27
Venue for Counting Electoral Votes 27
Opening of the Votes. 27
Reading of the Votes by House and Senate Tellers 27
Counting the Votes and Announcing the Result 28
Expediting the Process of Opening and Reading Votes. 28
The Majority Required for Election 28
Procedures for Conducting the Joint Session. 29
Objecting to the Counting of One or More Electoral Votes 30
Disposing of Objections 30
Procedures for Considering Objections 31
Basis for Objections. 31
Receipt of Two Certificates from the Same State 32
Electoral Vote Timetable and Subsequent Action 33

Presidential Transitions: Issues Involving Outgoing and Incoming Administrations. 34

Introduction. 35
Establishing a Presidential Transition Framework. 36
Presidential Transitions and National Security 37
Overview of Issues Related to Presidential Transitions. 37
Personnel—Political-to-Career Conversions ("Burrowing In"). 40
Appointments to Career Positions 41
Office of Personnel Management Approval 42
New Reporting Requirement for OPM 44
Government Accountability Office Review 44
Congressional Oversight 45
115th Congress. 45
114th Congress. 46
Issues for Congressional Consideration 48
Government Records. 49

From Election to Inauguration—An Overview of the Process v

Federal Records 49
A New Definition for Federal Records 50
Administration Recordkeeping Guidance and Requirements 51
NARA's Administration Transition Bulletins 52
Presidential Records 53
Amendments to the Presidential Records Act 54
Growth in Records and Volume 54
Executive Clemency 56
Background 56
Possible Congressional Concerns 57
Acts of Clemency Might Restrict Oversight of the Executive Branch 57
Acts of Clemency Might Have Implications for U.S. Foreign Relations 57
Cybersecurity Issues 58
Cybersecurity Incident Coordination 58
Positions with Cybersecurity Responsibilities 59
National Security Considerations and Options 60
Risks Accompanying the Presidential Transition Period 61
Presidential Transition Period Considerations 61
Congressional and Executive Branch Options 62
Agency Rulemaking 63
Overview of Midnight Rulemaking 63
Regulatory Moratoria and Postponements 64
Options for Congress: Oversight of Midnight Rules 65
Congressional Review Act 65
Appropriations Provisions 66
Executive Branch Political Appointments into the Next Presidency 68
Appointment Authority for Officers of the United States 68
Tenure during a Transition for a Confirmed Appointee 69
Tenure during a Transition for a Recess Appointee 70
Judicial Branch Appointments 71
Vacancies Awaiting a New President 71
Timing of Nominations Made by a New President 72
Executive Orders 73
Timing and Volume of Executive Orders 74
Content of Executive Orders 76
Submission of the President's Budget in Transition Years 77
Is the Outgoing or Incoming President Required to Submit the Budget? 77
Transition Year Budgets: Deadlines and Timing of Recent Submissions 78
Transition Year Budgets: Special Messages and Budget Revisions 79

Appendix A. Electoral Vote Allocation by States and District of Columbia 80

Appendix B. Federal Election Results: Frequently Asked Questions . 82

Introduction 83
What is the difference between returns reported on election night and final results? 85

How do states finalize election results? 85
What procedures might election jurisdictions use to provide transparency and
    demonstrate that the canvass is conducted correctly? 87
What processes help election officials determine voter eligibility and the validity of
    ballots cast? 88
When do states count ballots and certify election results? 91
How might the COVID-19 pandemic affect vote count procedures and timing in 2020?.... 92
How have states responded to potential effects of COVID-19 on the 2020 vote count? ... 93
What processes are available if disputes remain after election results are certified?........ 94

Appendix C. Supreme Court Clarifies Rules for Electoral College: States May Restrict Faithless Electors......................96

Background.. 96
Supreme Court Decision 97
Implications for Congress 98

The Electoral College: How It Works in Contemporary Presidential Elections

May 15, 2017   RL32611

When Americans vote for a President and Vice President, they are actually choosing presidential electors, known collectively as the electoral college. It is these officials who choose the President and Vice President of the United States. The complex elements comprising the electoral college system are responsible for election of the President and Vice President.

The 2016 presidential contest was noteworthy for the first *simultaneous* occurrence in presidential election history of four rarely occurring electoral college eventualities. These included (1) the election of a President and Vice President who received fewer popular votes than their major opponents; (2) the actions of seven "faithless electors," who voted for candidates other than those to whom they were pledged; (3) the split allocation of electoral votes in Maine, which uses the district system to allocate electors; and (4) objections to electoral votes at the joint session of Congress to count the votes. These events are examined in detail in the body of this report.

Article II, Section 1 of the Constitution, as modified in 1804 by the Twelfth Amendment, sets the requirements for election of the President and Vice President. It authorizes each state to appoint, by whatever means the legislature chooses, a number of electors equal to the combined total of its Senate and House of Representatives delegations, for a contemporary total of 538, including 3 electors for the District of Columbia. For over 150 years, the states have universally required that electors be chosen by the voters. Anyone may serve as an elector, except Members of Congress and persons holding offices of "Trust or Profit" under the Constitution.

Every presidential election year, political parties and independent candidacies nominate their national candidates for President and Vice President. In each state where they are entitled to be on the ballot, they also nominate a group (a "slate" or "ticket") of candidates for the office of elector that is equal in number to the electoral votes to which the state is entitled.

Introduction

The President and Vice President of the United States are chosen indirectly by a group of persons elected by America's voters. These officials are known as electors, and the institution is referred to collectively as the electoral college. Article II, Section 1 of the Constitution (1787), as modified by the Twelfth Amendment (1804), provides the constitutional framework for the process, which, together with an array of subsequent federal and state laws and political party practices, comprises the electoral college system as it exists today. It has been criticized by some as an undemocratic anachronism, but praised by others as a pillar of political stability and American federalism.

This report focuses on the institutions and procedures associated with the contemporary electoral college system. It opens by noting four rarely occurring electoral college eventualities that took place in connection with the 2016 presidential election. These included the election of a President and Vice President who received fewer popular votes than their major opponents; the actions of seven "faithless electors," who voted for candidates other than those to whom they were pledged; the split allocation of electoral votes in Maine, which uses the district system to choose its electors; and challenges to electoral votes in the joint session of Congress at which they are counted.

The report also examines the constitutional origins of the electoral college system and identifies the additional components and processes that are the product of federal and state law, party requirements, and political tradition, explaining their role in presidential elections. It provides a timeline for operation of the electoral college system for the 2020 presidential election, a brief examination of alternative reform measures, including constitutional amendment proposals and non-governmental initiatives, such as the National Popular Vote initiative[1] (NPV), and closes with concluding observations on the state of the electoral college system and prospects for change.

Most Recent Developments: The Electoral College and the 2016 Presidential Election

The 2016 presidential election will be recorded as the first in modern history in which four electoral college eventualities that have occurred separately in the past occurred during the same election cycle.

The Electoral and Popular Votes: Different Results

The President and Vice President were elected with a majority of electoral votes, but fewer popular votes than their major party opponents.[2] The 2016 election marked the fourth occurrence

---

[1] The National Popular Vote initiative is examined later in this report, under "Criticisms and Reform Proposals in Brief." It is also the subject of CRS Report R43823, *The National Popular Vote Initiative: Direct Election of the President by Interstate Compact*, by (name redacted) and (name redacted).

[2] Republican Party nominees Donald Trump and Mike Pence won 304 electoral votes, a majority of 56.5%, while Democratic Party nominees Hillary Clinton and Tim Kaine won 227 electoral votes, 42.2% of the total. Conversely, Clinton and Kaine won 65,853,516 popular votes, a plurality of 48.18% of the popular vote total, while Trump and Pence won 62,984,825 popular votes, 46.09% of the total. Other candidates won seven electoral votes, 1.3% of the electoral vote total, and 7,830,896 popular votes, 5.73% of the total. Source: U.S. Federal Election Commission, *Official 2016 Presidential Election Results*, January 30, 2017, at http://www.fec.gov/pubrec/fe2016/2016presgeresults.pdf.

of this eventuality, which occurred previously in 1876, 1888, and 2000. This election result is sometimes referred to, particularly by proponents of electoral college reform, as a "wrong winner" election or an "electoral college misfire."[3] This eventuality stemmed directly from the constitutional structure of the electoral college system. Article II, Section 1 of the Constitution and its Twelfth Amendment require a majority of electoral votes to elect the President and Vice President, but they contain no reference at all to popular votes.

Faithless Electors

Seven electors—five Democrats and two Republicans—cast votes for candidates other than those to whom they were pledged.[4] This phenomenon, generally referred to as "faithless" or "unfaithful" electors, also derives directly from the Constitution, which in the Twelfth Amendment, instructs electors to "vote by ballot for President and Vice President." While tradition that electors reflect the popular vote exerts a strong influence, there is no constitutional requirement that they vote for the candidates to whom they are pledged.

Maine Splits Its Electoral Vote

For the first time since it adopted the "district system" to award electors, the electoral vote in Maine was split between the two major party tickets—Republican nominees Trump and Pence received one vote for the district they carried and Democratic nominees Clinton and Kaine received three, one for the district they won and two at-large electors for winning the statewide popular vote.[5] This eventuality also has constitutional origins, since Article II, Section 1 authorizes the states to appoint their electors "in such Manner as the legislature thereof may direct." The only other modern instance of the district system producing split electoral votes occurred in Nebraska in 2008.[6]

Unsuccessful Objection in the Joint Electoral Vote Count Session

Title 3, Section 15 of the U.S. Code, which includes procedures for the counting of electoral votes in Congress, provides for objections to state certificates of electoral votes at the joint session of Congress at which electoral votes are counted. Several Members of the House of Representatives raised objections to electoral votes at the January 6, 2017, joint session of Congress at which the votes were counted. These objections were not considered, however, because they did not meet the legal requirements, which include signatures from at least one Senator and one Representative.[7]

---

[3] See, for instance, David W. Abbott and James P. Levine, *Wrong Winner, The Coming Debacle in the Electoral College* (New York, Praeger, 1991), Neal R. Peirce and Lawrence D. Longley, *The People's President, The Electoral College in American History and the Direct Vote Alternative*, revised edition (New Haven, CT: Yale University Press, 1980), "Chances of a Misfire," pp. 116-119.

[4] Federal Election Commission, *Official 2016 Presidential Election Results*, January 30, 2017, at http://www.fec.gov/pubrec/fe2016/2016presgeresults.pdf.

[5] Maine, Secretary of State, *Tabulations for Elections Held in 2016*, at http://maine.gov/sos/cec/elec/results/results16-17.html#tally.

[6] At present, Maine and Nebraska are the only two states that award electoral votes by the district system. For further information, see in this report "The District System," pp. 11-12.

[7] 3 U.S.C. §15. For proceedings at the joint count session of January 6, 2017, please consult *Congressional Record*, daily edition, volume 163, number 4, pp. H185-H190.

Public Opinion and the Electoral College: Post-2016 Election Developments

In addition to these eventualities, the Gallup Organization measured a change in public support for the electoral college system—versus direct popular election—immediately following the 2016 presidential election.

Public opinion has consistently and historically favored direct popular election over retention of the electoral college, with support for direct popular election never previously falling below 58%, as measured by Gallup since 1967. In January 2013, for instance, the Gallup Poll reported that 63% of respondents favored a constitutional amendment providing for direct popular election, while 29% favored retention of the electoral college.[8]

Following the 2016 election, however, the Gallup Poll reported a rise in support levels for the electoral college; according to poll results published on December 2, 2016, 49% of respondents favored an amendment providing for direct popular election, while 47% favored retention of the electoral college.[9] According to Gallup, this change was due to the fact that "[i]n the aftermath of this year's election, the percentage of Republicans wanting to replace the Electoral College with the popular vote has fallen significantly."[10] Specifically, support for direct election by respondents who identified themselves as "Republican" or "Republican-leaning Independents" fell from 54% in 2012 to 19% following the 2016 election. Conversely, levels of support for direct popular election among "Democratic or Democratic-leaning" respondents rose to new heights, from 69% in 2012 to 81% in 2016.[11]

Constitutional Origins

The Constitutional Convention of 1787 considered several methods of electing the President, including selection by Congress, by the governors of the states, by the state legislatures, by a special group of Members of Congress chosen by lot, and by direct popular election. None of these alternatives, however, proved satisfactory to the convention delegates. Late in the convention, the matter was referred to the Committee of Eleven on Postponed Matters, which devised the electoral college system in its original form.[12] This plan, which met with widespread approval by the delegates, was incorporated into the final document with only minor changes. As devised by the committee, the electoral college met several standards. It sought to

- reconcile and balance differing state and federal interests;
- give the state legislatures the authority to provide their preferred means of choosing the electors, including by popular vote, selection by the legislature itself, or any other method;

---

[8] Lydia Saad, "Americans Call for Term Limits, End to Electoral College," *The Gallup Poll*, January 18, 2013, at, http://www.gallup.com/poll/159881/americans-call-term-limits-end-electoral-college.aspx.

[9] Art Swift, "Americans' Support for Electoral College Rises Sharply," *The Gallup Poll*, December 2, 2016, at http://www.gallup.com/poll/198917/americans-support-electoral-college-rises-sharply.aspx.

[10] Ibid.

[11] Ibid.

[12] Although the term is not found in the Constitution, the electors have been known collectively as the electoral college since the early days of the republic, an expression that may be misleading, since the college has no continuing existence, never meets in plenary session, and ceases to exist immediately after the electors have performed their function.

- by providing the "constant two" "senatorial" or at-large electors, afford the "smaller" states some additional leverage, so the election process would not be totally dominated by the more populous states;
- preserve the presidency as independent of Congress for election and reelection; and
- generally insulate the election process from political manipulation.

In the final analysis, the electoral college method of electing the President and Vice President was perhaps the best deal the delegates felt they could get—seemingly the only one on which a consensus could be formed—and one of many compromises that contributed to the convention's success. Alexander Hamilton expressed the delegates' satisfaction with the electoral college method, and perhaps reflected their relief at reaching an acceptable solution, when he wrote this of the electoral college in *The Federalist:*

> The mode of appointment of the Chief Magistrate of the United States is almost the only part of the system, of any consequence, which has escaped without severe censure, or which has received the slightest mark of approbation from its opponents.... I venture somewhat further, and hesitate not to affirm that if the manner of it be not perfect, it is at least excellent. It united in an eminent degree all the advantages the union of which was to be wished for.[13]

The Original Constitutional System

The Constitution gave each state a number of electors equal to the combined total of its Senate and House of Representatives membership.[14] The electors were to be chosen by the states "in such Manner as the Legislature thereof may direct" (Article II, Section 1). Qualifications for the office were broad: the only persons prohibited from serving as electors are Senators, Representatives, and persons "holding an Office of Trust or Profit under the United States."[15]

In order to forestall partisan intrigue and manipulation, each state's electors were required to assemble separately in their respective states to cast their ballots rather than meet as a body in a single location.[16]

At least one of the candidates for whom the electors voted was required to be an inhabitant of another state. This was intended to counter what the framers feared would be a provincial insularity once George Washington, the indispensable figure who was universally expected to be the first President, had left the political scene. By requiring one of the candidates to be from somewhere else, the convention delegates hoped to prod the electors to look beyond the borders of their own state or region in search of national candidates qualified and fit to serve as President.

A number of votes equal to a majority of the whole number of electors was necessary to elect. This requirement was intended to insure that the winning candidate enjoyed broad support, while election by the House of Representatives was provided as a default method in the event of electoral college deadlock. Finally, Congress was empowered to set nationwide dates for choice and meeting of electors.

---

[13] Alexander Hamilton, "The Method of Electing the President," in *The Federalist*, number 68 (Cambridge, MA: Belknap Press of Harvard U. Press, 1966), p. 440.

[14] A map and table portraying the current allocation of electoral votes among the states may be found in the **Appendix** to this report, on pages 22-23.

[15] U.S. Constitution, Article II, Section 1, clause 2.

[16] Hamilton, "The Method of Electing the President," p. 440.

The Twelfth Amendment Repairs Flaws in the Original System

The original method of electing the President and Vice President, however, proved unworkable. Under this system, each elector cast two votes for two different candidates for the office of *President*, but no votes for *Vice President*. The candidate who received the most electoral votes was elected, provided he received a number of votes equal to a majority of the whole number of *electors*—not a majority of *electoral votes*. Nobody actually ran for Vice President—the runner-up in the presidential contest was elected to the second office. This system, which was intended to bring the two best qualified candidates to office, never anticipated the early growth of political parties and factions, each of which offered a joint ticket of two candidates—one for President and one for Vice President.

By the third election, in 1796, the nascent political parties of the day, Federalists and anti-Federalists (also known as Jeffersonians or Republicans),[17] each offered a joint ticket. Under the original arrangement, the only way to make the system work was for all of the party's electors to cast one of their two votes for the recognized presidential candidate, and *all but one* of the electors cast their second votes for the vice presidential candidate. One elector would be instructed to withhold his second vote for the designated vice presidential candidate, so that the two candidates would not tie the vote and throw the election to the House.

This cumbersome system broke down almost immediately, in 1800, when a Republican elector failed to withhold his second vote from the acknowledged vice presidential candidate. This led to a tie between presidential candidate Thomas Jefferson and his running mate, Aaron Burr, leaving the election to be decided in the House of Representatives. The constitutional crisis resulting from the election of 1800 led to the Twelfth Amendment, which was proposed by Congress and speedily ratified by the states, as noted later in this report.[18]

The Electoral College Today[19]

Notwithstanding the founders' efforts, the electoral college system almost never functioned as they intended, but, as with so many constitutional provisions, the document prescribed only the system's basic elements, leaving ample room for development. As the republic evolved, so did the electoral college system; by the late 19th century the following range of constitutional requirements, federal and state legal provisions, and political party practices that make up the contemporary system were in place.

---

[17] To avoid confusion, it should be noted that the "Jeffersonian" or "Republican" proto-party of the 1790s was the ancestor of the modern Democratic Party. The modern Republican Party, which also claimed descent from the Jeffersonians, emerged in the 1850s.

[18] For further information on the election of 1800 and the Twelfth Amendment, see Peirce and Longley, *The People's President,* revised edition, pp. 36-44.

[19] For information on electoral college reform, please consult CRS Report R43824, *Electoral College Reform: Contemporary Issues for Congress*, by (name redacted) , and CRS Report R43823, *The National Popular Vote Initiative: Direct Election of the President by Interstate Compact*, by (name redacted) and (name redacted).

From Election to Inauguration—An Overview of the Process 7

Who Are the Electors?[20]

The Constitution, as noted earlier in this report, states what the electors *may not be*; that is, it prohibits Senators, Representatives, and persons holding an "Office of Trust or Profit under the United States" from serving. In effect, this language bars not only Members of the two houses of Congress, but any person who is an employee of the United States government: Justices, judges, and staff of the U.S. courts and the federal judiciary; all political employees of the legislative and executive branches; civilian employees of the U.S. Government, that is, "civil servants," and U.S. military and law enforcement personnel.[21]

In practice, the two major political parties in each state tend to nominate a mixture of well-known figures such as governors and other state and local elected officials, party activists, local and state celebrities, and "ordinary" citizens for the office of elector.

While they may be well-known persons in their states, electors generally receive little recognition as such. In most states, the names of individual elector-candidates do not appear anywhere on the ballot; instead only those of the presidential and vice presidential candidates of the parties or other groups that nominated the elector-candidates appear. In some states, the presidential and vice-presidential nominees' names are preceded on the ballot by the words "electors for." The usual anonymity of presidential electors is such that electoral votes are commonly referred to as having "been awarded" to the winning candidates, as if no human beings were involved in the process.

Nominating Elector-Candidates: Diverse State Procedures

The Constitution and federal law are silent on nomination procedures for elector-candidates, so the process of nominating elector-candidates is another of the aspects of this system left to state and political party preferences. Most states prescribe one of two methods: 32 states and the District of Columbia provide by law that major party candidates for presidential elector be nominated by state party conventions, while five states provide by law for nomination by the state party's central committee. The remaining states use a variety of methods; for instance, some make no provision for nomination of elector-candidates, leaving the decision to party authorities. Others provide for nomination by the governor (on recommendation of party committees), by primary election, and by the party's presidential nominee. Provisions governing new and minor political parties, as well as independent candidacies, are generally prescribed in state law, and are even more widely varied.[22]

---

[20] For Certificates of Ascertainment that include names of each state's 2016 presidential electors, please consult the National Archives and Records Administration's website at https://www.archives.gov/federal-register/electoral-college/2016/certificates-of-ascertainment.html.

[21] It is unclear whether the constitutional prohibition covers persons who serve without compensation on federal executive or congressional advisory boards and commissions. A 2007 opinion for the General Counsel of the Federal Bureau of Investigation (FBI) held that members of the FBI Director's Advisory Board should not be considered to hold an "Office of Profit or Trust" under the United States, as described in the Constitution's so-called emoluments clause (Article I, Section 9, clause 8). From this opinion, it could be inferred that members of the said boards and commissions would not be covered by the Article II, Section 1, clause 2 prohibiting persons holding "an Office of Trust or Profit" from serving as presidential electors. For further information, consult "Application of the Emoluments Clause to a Member of the Federal Bureau of Investigation Director's Advisory Board," Memorandum Opinion for the General Counsel, Federal Bureau of Investigation, June 15, 2007, at http://www.justice.gov/sites/default/files/olc/opinions/2007/06/31/fbi_advisory_board_opinion_061507_0.pdf.

[22] For information on elector-nomination procedures in the individual states, please consult: U.S. Congress, *Nomination and Election of the President and Vice President of the United States, 2008*, 111th Congress 2nd sess., S. Doc. 111-15 (continued...)

How Are Electoral Votes Allocated Among the States?

The Constitution, as noted previously, gives each state a number of electors equal to the combined total of its Senate membership (2 for each state) and House of Representatives delegation (currently ranging from 1 to 53, depending on population).[23] The Twenty-third Amendment provides an additional 3 electors to the District of Columbia. The total number of electoral votes per state, based on the most recent (2010) census, ranges from 3, for seven states and the District of Columbia, to 55 for California, the most populous state. **Figure A-1** and **Table A-1** in the appendix to this report provide current electoral vote allocations by state and the District of Columbia for the elections of 2012, 2016, and 2020.

These totals are adjusted following each decennial census in a process called reapportionment, which reallocates the number of Members of the House of Representatives to reflect changing rates of population growth or decline among the states.[24] Thus, a state may gain or lose electors following reapportionment, as it gains or loses Representatives, but it always retains its two "senatorial" or at-large electors, and at least one more reflecting its House delegation. As noted previously, the current allocation among the states is in effect for the presidential elections of 2012, 2016, and 2020; electoral votes will next be reallocated following the 2020 census, an alignment that will be in effect for the 2024 and 2028 elections.

How Are the Electors Chosen?

As also noted previously, the Constitution specifically grants the right to decide how electors will be *chosen*—as opposed to being *nominated*—to the legislatures of the several states:

> Each State shall appoint, in such Manner as the Legislature thereof may direct, a Number of Electors, equal to the whole Number of Senators and Representatives to which the State may be entitled in the Congress.[25]

In the early days of the republic, the legislatures themselves chose presidential electors in more than half the states, which meant that the voters in those states had no direct involvement in the election. This practice changed rapidly, however, as "the rise of democratic sentiment in the early nineteenth century"[26] led to the steady expansion of voting rights to include all white males 21 years of age or older. By 1832, choice of presidential electors had changed from the legislatures to the voters in every state but one, and since 1864 the voters have chosen electors in all states, a tradition that has become a permanent feature of the electoral college system.[27]

Today, while the citizens vote for the presidential electors, the constitutional authority of the state legislatures to decide how they will be chosen as set forth in Article II, Section 1 continues to be in effect.[28] This was illustrated as recently as 2000. During the political controversy connected

---

(...continued)

(Washington: GPO, 2010), pp. 346-428. This is the most recent edition available in 2017.

[23] U.S. Constitution, Article II, Section 1, clause 2.

[24] For additional information on the apportionment process, please consult CRS Report R41357, *The U.S. House of Representatives Apportionment Formula in Theory and Practice*, by (name redacted)

[25] U.S. Constitution, Article II, Section 1, clause 2.

[26] Peirce and Longley, *The People's President,* revised edition, p. 45.

[27] Ibid., pp. 44-47. Today, the right to vote is guaranteed to all qualified persons eighteen years of age or older by the Fourteenth, Fifteenth, Nineteenth, Twenty-fourth, and Twenty-sixth Amendments to the Constitution, and legislation such as the Voting Rights Act as Amended (52 U.S.C. §10101-10702).

[28] The legislature's power is, however, subject to certain constitutional constraints, particularly if state procedures are (continued...)

with that year's presidential election in Florida, it was suggested that the state's legislature might step in to appoint electors if local election authorities and state courts were unable to determine who had won its 25 electoral votes by the deadline required by federal law (this so-called "Safe Harbor" provision is examined later in this report). Although many commentators asserted that a return to selection of electors by the state legislature would be an unacceptable retreat from democratic practices, no serious arguments were raised against the constitutional right of the Florida legislature to do so.[29]

The Electors' Task: Ratifying the Voters' Choice

Presidential electors in contemporary elections are expected, and, in many cases pledged, to vote for the candidates of the party that nominated them. While there is considerable evidence that the founders intended that they would be independent, weighing the merits of competing presidential candidates, the electors have been regarded as agents of the public will since the first decade under the Constitution.[30] They are expected to vote for the candidates of the party that nominated them. "Faithless" electors provide an occasional exception to that accepted rule.

Faithless Electors: Disregarding the Voters' Choice

Notwithstanding the tradition that electors are bound to vote for the candidates of the party that nominated them, individual electors have sometimes broken their commitment, voting for a different candidate or for candidates other than those to whom they were pledged; they are known as "faithless" or "unfaithful" electors. Although 24 states seek to prohibit faithless electors by a variety of methods, including pledges and the threat of fines or criminal action,[31] most constitutional scholars believe that once electors have been chosen, they remain constitutionally free agents, able to vote for any candidate who meets the requirements for President and Vice President.[32] Faithless electors have been few in number prior to 2016: since 1900, there have been eight, one each in the elections of 1948, 1956, 1960, 1968, 1972, 1976, 1988 and 2004,[33] and one

---

(...continued)

found to have violated the equal protection clause of the Fourteenth Amendment. For additional information, please consult U.S. Congress, Senate, *The Constitution of the United States, Analysis and Interpretation*, "Article II, Section 1, clauses 2-4," 108th Cong., 2nd sess., Sen. Doc. 108-17 (Washington: GPO, 2004), pp. 450-452. Also available online at http://www.gpo.gov/fdsys/search/pagedetails.action?granuleId=GPO-CONAN-2002-8-3&packageId=GPO-CONAN-2002&fromBrowse=true.

[29] Jim Saunders and Randolph Pendleton, "Legislators Poised to Pick Bush Electors," *Florida Times Union/Jacksonville.com*, December 12, 2000, available at http://jacksonville.com/tu-online/stories/121200/met_4857971.html; and John C. Fortier, ed., *After the People Vote, A Guide to the Electoral College*, third edition, (Washington: AEI Press, 2005), p. 45.

[30] Peirce and Longley, *The People's President*, revised edition, pp. 24, 96-101.

[31] For information on these restrictions, please consult: U.S. Congress, *Nomination and Election of the President and Vice President of the United States, 2008*, pp. 346-428. This is the most recent edition available in 2017.

[32] U.S. Congress, Senate, *The Constitution of the United States of America, Analysis and Interpretation*, pp. 453-455. Also available in PDF format at https://www.gpo.gov/fdsys/pkg/GPO-CONAN-2002/pdf/GPO-CONAN-2002.pdf.

[33] 1948-1988: FairVote website, "Faithless Electors," This source provided the names of faithless electors, where available, and the circumstances under which they cast their votes, at http://www.fairvote.org/faithless_electors. 2004: In 2004, one Minnesota elector cast votes for John Edwards for both President and Vice President. No objection was raised in the January 6, 2005, joint session at which electoral votes were counted, and the vote was recorded as cast. See National Archives and Records Administration website, "Historical Election Results," at http://www.archives.gov/federal-register/electoral-college/scores2.html#2004.

blank ballot cast in 2000.[34] They have never influenced the outcome of a presidential election, however, but prior to 2016, their "faithless" votes, or failure to vote, were all duly recorded.[35]

2016: Faithless Electors—Ten Attempted, Seven Successful

Following the 2016 presidential election, 10 electors attempted to cast ballots for candidates other than those to whom they were pledged; seven succeeded. Three Clinton-Kaine electors—from Colorado, Maine, and Minnesota—attempted to vote for other candidates, but they were replaced by alternates who cast their ballots as electors according to the voters' preference.[36] Seven electors, however, successfully cast votes for candidates other than those chosen by their state's voters in the popular election. These included electors from three states:

- **Hawaii**—one Clinton-Kaine elector voted for Bernie Sanders for President and Elizabeth Warren for Vice President;
- **Texas**—two Trump-Pence electors cast one vote each for President for John Kasich and Ron Paul, one vote for Vice President for Carly Fiorina, but one of these electors cast no ballot for Vice President; and
- **Washington**—four Clinton-Kaine electors cast three votes for President for Colin Powell and one vote for President for Faith Spotted Eagle, and one vote each for Vice President for Elizabeth Warren, Maria Cantwell, Susan Collins, and Winona LaDuke.[37]

This was the largest number since 1836 of electors who voted for candidates other than those for whom the voters in their states cast ballots.[38] In December 2016, as provided by Washington law, the Secretary of State of that state fined the four electors who had voted against the popular vote winners. The fines were subsequently upheld by a state administrative law judge.[39]

General Election Ballots

General election ballots, which are regulated by state election laws and authorities, offer voters joint candidacies for President and Vice President for each political party or other group on the ballot. That is, voters cast a single vote for electors pledged to the joint ticket of the presidential and vice presidential nominees of the party they represent. This practice conforms to the Constitution, which provides for only one set of electors, although the electors vote separately for President and Vice President. This practice eliminates the possibility that voters could pick and choose among electors from different parties. The joint ticket also ensures that the President and Vice President will represent the same party.

---

[34] For the name of the elector and the circumstances under which this elector cast a blank electoral vote ballot in 2000, see ibid., at http://www.fairvote.org/faithless_electors.

[35] National Archives and Records Administration website, "Who Are the Electors?" at http://www.archives.gov/federal-register/electoral-college/electors.html#restrictions.

[36] Scott Detrow, "Donald Trump Secures Electoral Win with Few Surprises," NPR (National Public Radio), December 19, 2016, at http://www.npr.org/2016/12/19/506188169/donald-trump-poised-to-secure-electoral-college-win-with-few-surprises.

[37] *Congressional Record*, daily edition, volume 163, number 4, January 6, 2017, p. H-189.

[38] In 1836, all 23 Virginia electors voted against instructions in the vice presidential contest. For information on faithless electors in earlier elections, see Fairvote, "Faithless Electors," at http://www.fairvote.org/faithless_electors.

[39] Reid Wilson, "Washington Judge Upholds Fine for Faithless Electors," *The Hill*, March 9, 2017, at http://thehill.com/homenews/state-watch/323124-wash-judge-upholds-fines-for-faithless-electors.

Most states do not print the names of individual elector-candidates on the general election ballot. The most common practice is that only the names of the presidential and vice presidential nominees and their party identification appear on the ballot, in some cases preceded by the phrase "Electors for". Some states further specify in law that a vote for these candidates is a vote for the elector-candidates of their party or political group.[40]

The General Ticket and District Systems: How the States Award Their Electoral Votes

While the Constitution is silent on the exact procedure for awarding each state's electoral votes, 48 states and the District of Columbia currently use the "general ticket" or "winner-take-all" system, while Maine and Nebraska use the "district" system.

The General Ticket System

Under the general ticket system, also referred to as the winner-take-all system, each political party or independent candidacy that is eligible to be placed on the ballot nominates a group (also known as "ticket" or "slate") of candidates for the office of elector. The number of candidates for the office of elector nominated by each party on its ticket equals the state's total number of electors. As noted previously, the voters then cast a single vote for the presidential and vice presidential candidates of their choice; when they do, they actually cast a vote for the entire ticket of electors pledged to the party and candidates of their choice. Again, under the general ticket/winner-take all system, all the elector-candidates on the ticket receiving the most votes statewide[41] are elected as presidential and vice presidential electors for that state.

The general ticket system has been favored since the 19th century, because it awards all the state's electors to one party's nominees, thus tending to magnify the winning candidates' victory margin within states and across the nation. Historically, it has usually produced an electoral college majority for the winners greater than the percentage of their popular vote margin of victory. This recurring development is sometimes referred to as a "multiplier effect." As Neal Peirce and Lawrence Longley wrote in *The People's President*:

> ... the general ticket system suited the purposes of the ruling political faction in any state. No longer would it be necessary (as under the district system) to share the state's electoral votes with the opposing party. By the general ticket system, the ruling party could deliver an absolutely solid electoral vote majority to its national candidates.[42]

The 1960 presidential election offers a notable example of the general ticket multiplier effect. In that election, Democratic nominees John F. Kennedy and Lyndon B. Johnson won 49.72% of the popular vote, compared to 49.56% for Republican nominees Richard M. Nixon and Henry C. Lodge, a popular vote victory margin of 0.18%. This margin, however, was expanded in the electoral college by the effect of the general ticket system multiplier. The Democratic nominees thus gained 303 electoral votes, 56.42% of the total, to the Republican ticket's 219 electoral

---

[40] For information on individual state ballot format, please consult: U.S. Congress, *Nomination and Election of the President and Vice President of the United States, 2008*, pp. 346-428. This is the most recent edition available in 2017.

[41] A plurality of the popular vote is sufficient win all electoral votes in general ticket states, and the at-large electoral votes in district system states.

[42] Peirce and Longley, *The People's President*, revised edition, pp. 110-112.

votes, 40.78% of the total, an electoral college victory margin of 15.64%, or 86 times larger than the margin separating their respective popular vote totals.[43]

How Does the General Ticket System Work?

This is how the general ticket system would work in hypothetical "State A" in a contemporary presidential election. State A currently has 10 electoral votes, reflecting its 2 Senators and 8 Representatives. Assume that two parties are eligible to appear on the ballot, "Party X" and "Party Y"; each nominates 10 persons for the office of elector, pledged to the presidential and vice presidential candidates nominated by their party. Voters go to the polls and cast *a single vote* for the "general ticket" of electors pledged to the candidates they support, although as noted previously, only the names of the presidential and vice presidential candidates are likely to appear on the ballot. Assuming that Party X's ticket of elector-candidates receives 51% of the popular vote, and Party Y's ticket receives 49%, *then all 10 of Party X's electors are chosen—"winner-take-all"*—and Party Y wins *no* electoral votes in the state. The Party X electors are pledged to their party's presidential and vice presidential candidates, and they normally vote to confirm the choice of the citizens who elected them.

The District System

The district system is a variation that has been adopted by Maine and Nebraska. Under this arrangement, the voters in each state choose

- two electors on a statewide, at-large basis (representing the two senatorial or at-large electors allotted to each state regardless of population); and
- one elector in each congressional district.[44]

Each voter still casts a single vote for President and Vice President, but the votes are counted twice: first on a statewide basis, where the two at-large elector-candidates who win the most votes (a plurality is sufficient) are both elected, and then again in each district, where the district elector-candidate who receives the most votes in each district (again, a plurality is sufficient) is elected.

How Does the District System Work?

This is how the district system might work in the same hypothetical State A, which, as noted previously is apportioned 8 Representatives in Congress; when its 2 senatorial or at-large electors are added, it has 10 electors. In this scenario, Party X again receives 51% of the statewide vote, and Party Y receives 49%. Under the district system, therefore, Party X's candidates for the two senatorial or at-large electors are elected, because Party X won the statewide popular vote. The remaining electors are chosen on a district basis. For the district electors, assume that Party X receives a plurality or majority of the popular vote in five of State A's eight congressional districts, while Party Y wins in the other three districts. Under the district system, these electors are awarded to the popular vote winners in each particular district, so that Party X, having won

---

[43] Computed by CRS from Rhodes Cook et al., *America Votes 28, Election Returns by State, 2007-2008* (Washington, CQ Press: 2010), pp, 41-42. In 1960, six Democratic electors in Alabama and one in Oklahoma voted for candidates other than those to whom they were pledged, while eight "unpledged Democratic" electors in Mississippi cast their votes for persons other than their party's nominees.

[44] Some proposed versions of the district system would use ad hoc presidential election districts to award these votes, rather than congressional districts, but both Maine and Nebraska tally their votes by congressional district.

five districts, would receive five district votes, which, when added to the senatorial or at-large electors, would total seven electors, while Party Y, having won three districts, would receive the three electors that reflected its congressional district victories. The total allocation of electoral votes would thus be two at-large electors and five district electors for Party X, a total of seven, and three district electors for Party Y, a total of three.

2016: The District System Produces a Divided Result in Maine

In the 2016 presidential election campaign, Democratic nominees Clinton and Kaine won the Maine statewide popular vote 48% to 45% over Republican nominees Trump and Pence, *and* the vote in the First Congressional District by 54% to 40%. Trump and Pence won the Second Congressional District by 51% to 41%. As the district system provides, Clinton and Kaine received three electors: two for their statewide total and one for winning the First District. Trump and Pence received one elector, representing their victory in the Second District.[45] Although the district system was more widely used in the early 19th century, at present, only Maine, since the 1972 election, and Nebraska, since 1992, award their electoral votes on this basis. The only other split in electoral votes in modern times occurred in Nebraska in 2008, when four votes were awarded to Republican nominees McCain and Palin, who won two congressional districts and the statewide vote, and one was awarded to Democratic nominees Obama and Biden, who won a single congressional district.[46]

General Election Day

Elections for all federal elected officials are held on the Tuesday after the first Monday in November in even-numbered years; presidential elections are held in every year divisible by four. In 2020, general election day will fall on November 3.[47] Congress selected the Tuesday after the second Monday in November in 1845;[48] previously, states held elections on different days between September and November, a practice that sometimes led to multiple voting across state lines and other fraudulent practices. By mandating a single presidential election day, Congress sought to eliminate such irregularities.

Other factors also contributed to Congress's choice of a November election day. By tradition, November was chosen because the harvest would have been gathered, and the nation's predominantly rural farm population could spare the time for a day-long trip to the county seat, where voting was usually conducted. The choice of Tuesday provided a full day's travel time between Sunday, which was widely observed as a day of worship and rest, and election day. The choice of Tuesday *after the first Monday* also avoided potential congestion at the county seat on the first day of the month, which was generally the day on which local courts convened, or on Wednesday, which was often market day. Finally, travel was also easier during this season of the year, before winter had set in, especially in northern states.[49]

---

[45] Edward D. Murphy, "Trump Takes 1 of Maine's 4 Electoral Votes, in a First for the State," *Portland (ME) Press Herald*, November 9, 2016, at http://www.pressherald.com/2016/11/08/mainers-take-matters-into-their-own-hands-after-bitter-presidential-campaign/.

[46] Nebraska, Secretary of State, *Official Results of the Nebraska General Election, November 4, 2008*, at http://www.sos.ne.gov/elec/pdf/2008%20General%20Canvass%20Book.pdf.

[47] 3 U.S.C. §1.

[48] *Statutes at Large*, 5 Stat. 721.

[49] Lily Rothman, "The Reason Election Day Is Tuesday," *Time*, November 2, 2015, at http://time.com/4089657/history-election-day/.

The Electors Convene and Vote

The Twelfth Amendment requires electors to meet "in their respective states." As noted previously, this provision was intended by the founders to deter "intrigue" and manipulation of the election, by having the state electoral college delegations meet simultaneously, but in separate locations. Federal law sets the first Monday after the second Wednesday in December as the date on which the electors meet. In 2020, the electors will convene on December 14.[50]

The same law set the "safe harbor" provision to govern disputed popular election returns in any state. When presidential election returns are disputed in any state, if that state, prior to election day, has established procedures to resolve such disputes, and if it has used these procedures to reach a decision as to the election result not less than six days before the date on which the electors are scheduled to meet, then that decision is final.[51]

The electors almost always meet in the state capital, usually in the capitol building or state house itself. They vote "by ballot"—paper ballot[52]—separately for President and Vice President. At least one of the candidates must be from another state, a provision retained from the original constitutional requirement; as noted previously, this was intended by the founders to promote the selection of nationally renowned candidates, and to prevent the electors from selecting exclusively "native sons."

The results are then endorsed, and copies are sent to the following officials:

- the Vice President of the United States (in the Vice President's capacity of President of the Senate);
- the state secretary of state or the comparable state officer;
- the Archivist of the United States; and
- the judge of the federal district court of the district in which the electors met.[53]

The electors then adjourn, and the electoral college ceases to exist until the next presidential election.

Congress Counts, Ascertains, and Declares the Vote

Aside from the presidential inauguration on January 20, the final step in the presidential election process is the counting, ascertainment, and declaration of the electoral votes in Congress.[54] Federal law directs the House of Representatives and the Senate to meet in joint session in the House chamber on January 6 of the year following the presidential election. For the 2020 presidential election, this day falls on Wednesday, January 6, 2021. Congress may, however, provide by law for a different date, a practice it traditionally follows when January 6 falls on a Sunday. This occurred most recently in 2013.[55]

---

[50] 3 U.S.C. §7.

[51] This requirement, found at 3 U.S.C. §5, was crucial in decisive allocation of Florida's electors in the 2000 presidential election.

[52] Twelfth Amendment. This provision has historically been interpreted to require paper ballots for President and Vice President.

[53] 3 U.S.C. §11.

[54] 3 U.S.C. §15-18.

[55] 3 U.S.C. §15. The action of scheduling or rescheduling an electoral count joint session is customarily accomplished by a joint resolution originating in the House. For example, the 2009 session was set by H.J.Res. 100, 110th Congress, (continued...)

From Election to Inauguration—An Overview of the Process 15

No debate is allowed in the joint session. The Vice President, who presides as President of the Senate, opens the electoral vote certificates from each state, in alphabetical order. The Vice President then passes the certificates to four tellers (vote counters), two appointed by the House, and two by the Senate, who announce the results. The votes are then counted, and the results are announced by the Vice President. The candidates who receive a majority of electoral votes, currently 270 of 538, are declared the winners by the Vice President, an action that constitutes "a sufficient declaration of the persons, if any, elected President and Vice President of the States."[56]

Objections to State Electoral Vote Returns

Objections may be offered to both individual electoral votes and state returns as a whole. Objections must be filed in writing, "state clearly and concisely, without argument, the ground thereof,"[57] and be signed by one U.S. Senator and one Representative. If an objection is received in the joint session, and is signed by one Senator and one Representative, then the electoral vote count session is recessed. The Senate returns immediately to its chamber, and the two houses of Congress consider the objections separately. Under federal law,[58] these sessions cannot last more than two hours, and no Member of either house may speak for more than five minutes. At the end of this period, the houses vote separately to agree or disagree with the objection. The Senate then returns to the House chamber, and the joint session reconvenes. The decisions of the two houses are announced. If both houses agree to the objection, then the electoral vote or votes in question are not counted. Otherwise, the vote or votes stand as submitted, and are counted as such.[59]

An objection that met the aforesaid criteria was filed most recently following the 2004 presidential election. The objection was made against the certificate of the electoral vote filed by the State of Ohio at the joint electoral count session held on January 6, 2005. It met the required standards, being submitted in writing, and bearing the signatures of one Representative and one Senator. The joint session was duly recessed, and the two houses of Congress reconvened separately to debate and vote on the objection, which they rejected. The certificate of electoral votes submitted by Ohio was accepted, and the vote was duly recorded.[60]

2016: Attempted Objections in the Joint Session to Count Electoral Votes

Following the 2016 presidential election, several Representatives attempted to file objections during the January 6, 2017, joint session to count electoral votes and declare the election results.

(...continued)

P.L. 110-430, 122 Stat. 4846. In 2013, January 6 fell on a Sunday, and the joint session was scheduled for Friday, January 4 by H.J.Res. 122, 112th Congress, P.L. 112-228, 126 Stat. 1610. January 6 will not fall again on a Sunday in a post-presidential election year until 2041. A date for the joint session to count electoral votes cast in the 2020 election will be set late in that year.

[56] 3 U.S.C. §15.

[57] Ibid.

[58] 3 U.S.C. §17.

[59] For further information on proceedings at joint electoral vote counting sessions of Congress, please consult CRS Report RL32717, *Counting Electoral Votes: An Overview of Procedures at the Joint Session, Including Objections by Members of Congress*, by (name redacted) and (name redacted)

[60] For the proceedings at the joint count session of January 6, 2005, please consult *Congressional Record*, volume 151, part 1, January 6, 2005, pp. 157-173, 197-243.

These were ruled out of order, however, because no Senator had signed the objection, and signatures of at least one Member of both chambers are required by the U.S. Code.[61]

A Tie or Failure to Win a Majority in the Electoral College: Contingent Election by Congress

The Twelfth Amendment, as noted earlier in this report, requires that candidates receive a majority of electoral votes, that is, at least 270 of the current total of 538, in order to be elected President or Vice President.

In the event of a tie, or if no candidate for either or both offices receives a majority, then choice of the President and Vice President "defaults" to Congress in a procedure known as contingent election.[62] In a contingent election, the House of Representatives elects the President, choosing from among the *three* candidates who received the most electoral votes. The House votes by state: each state delegation votes internally to decide for whom the state's vote shall be cast.[63] The Senate elects the Vice President in a contingent election, choosing between the *two* candidates who received the largest number of electoral votes. Unlike the House, each Senator casts an individual vote. For both offices, a majority is required to elect in a contingent election: 26 or more votes of individual states for President and 51 or more Senators' votes for Vice President. It should be noted that although the District of Columbia participates in presidential elections by choosing three electors, it would not participate in a contingent election for President or Vice President.[64]

Perhaps the most notable feature of contingent election is that each state casts an equal vote, regardless of population. In the House, each state delegation casts a single vote for President, while in the vice presidential election, each Senator casts a single vote.

Under the Twentieth Amendment, if the House of Representatives has been unable to elect a President prior to January 20 in a contingent election, then the Vice President-elect serves as acting President until the deadlock has been resolved. Congress may provide by law who will act as President if neither a President-elect nor a Vice President-elect has been chosen prior to January 20 in a contingent election procedure.

2020 Presidential Election: An Electoral College Timeline

This timeline for the 2020 presidential election relies on existing procedures governing the election process. It does not anticipate any major changes that might be effected between this time of this writing (May 2017) and then.

---

[61] For proceedings at the joint count session of January 6, 2017, please consult *Congressional Record*, daily edition, volume 163, number 4, pp. H185-H190.

[62] For further information, please consult CRS Report R40504, *Contingent Election of the President and Vice President by Congress: Perspectives and Contemporary Analysis*, by (name redacted) .

[63] In states represented by a single at-large Representative (Alaska, Delaware, Montana, North Dakota, South Dakota, Vermont and Wyoming), that Member would cast the state's vote for President in a contingent election.

[64] For further information, please consult Congressional Research Service Memorandum, *Would the District of Columbia Be Allowed to Vote in the Selection of the President by the House of Representatives?* by (name redacted), July 7, 1980. Available to Members of Congress and congressional staff from the author of this report.

May-August 2020—In each state, party organizations and other groups that are eligible to be included on the general election ballot, including minor parties and independent candidacies, will nominate a ticket of candidates for elector for President and Vice President in their states, following procedures outlined earlier in this report at "Nominating Elector-Candidates: Diverse State Procedures."

November 3, 2020—General Election Day. Voters cast one ballot for the joint ticket of their preferred candidates for President and Vice President. These are actually votes for the electors committed to those candidates.[65]

December 8, 2020—The "Safe Harbor" deadline. As noted earlier, if, on or before election day, a state has provided by law for determination of controversies or contests over the electors and electoral votes, and if these procedures have been applied, and results have been determined on or before this date, these results are considered to be conclusive, and will govern in the counting of the electoral votes.[66]

December 14, 2020—The electoral college meets. State delegations of electors meet separately in their respective states at a place designated by the state legislature. In practice, the electors usually meet in the state capital, often in the state house or capitol building. The electors vote "by ballot"—paper ballot—separately for President and Vice President. Certificates of the results are then transmitted to the President of the U.S. Senate (one copy), the Archivist of the United States (two copies), the secretary of state or equivalent officer of the state in which the electors met (two copies), and the judge of the U.S. district court of the district in which the electors met (one copy).[67]

December 23, 2020—Certificates must be delivered to the officers specified earlier in this report (see under "The Electors Convene and Vote") not later than the fourth Wednesday in December.[68]

January 6, 2021—On this date, or another date designated by Congress, the Senate and House of Representatives assemble in joint session to count the electoral votes. The announcement of the state of the vote is deemed sufficient declaration of the persons elected President and Vice president.[69]

January 20, 2021—The President and Vice President are inaugurated.[70]

Criticism and Defense of the Electoral College and Reform Proposals in Brief

The electoral college and the various federal and state laws and political party practices that comprise the nation's presidential election system have been subject to controversy from the earliest days under the Constitution.

---

[65] 3 U.S.C. §1.

[66] 3 U.S.C. §5.

[67] 3 U.S.C. §6-11.

[68] 3 U.S.C. §12, the fourth Wednesday in December

[69] 3 U.S.C. §15. In 2021, Since January 6, 2021, falls on a Wednesday, rather than a Sunday, Congress is less likely to reschedule the joint session to count electoral votes for another day.

[70] U.S. Constitution, Twentieth Amendment.

Criticisms

In the modern era, criticisms of the electoral college system center on various characteristics of the system, including, among others, the following:

- it provides for indirect election of the President and Vice President by electors allocated by state, rather than by direct nationwide popular vote;
- electors are not constitutionally required to follow the popular vote in their state;
- the general ticket system is said to disenfranchise those who voted for the losing candidates by awarding all the electors in a state to the winners and none to the losers;
- the general ticket system is also said contribute to elections—"electoral college misfires"—in which candidates may be elected with fewer popular votes than their opponents; and
- contingent election further removes the election from the voters by vesting it in the House and Senate and assigning the same vote to each state, notwithstanding differences in population.

Defense

Electoral college supporters cite a number of factors in their defense of the system, including the following:

- they reject the claim that it is undemocratic, noting that electors are chosen by the voters in free elections;
- the electoral college system, they assert, is a major component of American federalism, maintaining the Constitution prescribes a federal election by which votes are tallied in each state, and in which the voters act both as citizens of the United States, and members of their state communities;
- they also cite federalism in defense of the allocation of electors among the states, and call into question the validity of claims that various groups or political parties are advantaged under the system;
- defenders further maintain the electoral college has historically promoted broad-based electoral coalitions and moderate political parties; and
- they reject the faithless elector argument, noting that faithless electors have never influenced the outcome of an election.

Proposals for Change

Hundreds of constitutional amendments have been proposed to reform or eliminate the electoral college, falling into one of two categories: reform the system, "mend it," or replace it with direct popular election, "end it."

Electoral College Reform

Three alternative proposals to "mend it" have been the most widely proposed in the past:

- the automatic system; this would establish the general ticket system described earlier and currently used by 48 states and the District of Columbia as the mandatory nationwide system;
- the district system; this would establish the method currently used by Maine and Nebraska that allocates electoral votes on both a statewide and district basis, but as the mandatory nationwide system; and
- the proportional system, which would allocate electoral votes in each state according to the proportion of the popular votes won by each ticket in that state as the mandatory nationwide system.

All three of these reform proposals would retain electoral votes, but eliminate the office of elector, and thus eliminate the possibility of faithless electors.

Direct Popular Election

Under direct popular election, the candidates winning the most popular votes nationwide would be elected. Under most direct election proposals a simple plurality of the nationwide popular vote total would be sufficient to elect the President and Vice President, but some versions would set the plurality threshold at 40% of the popular vote, while others would require a majority to elect.[71]

Action in Congress on Electoral College Reform, 1940s-Present

From the late 1940s through 1979, Congress considered numerous electoral college reform measures. Constitutional amendments that proposed to reform or eliminate the system were the subject of hearings in the Senate and House Judiciary Committees on 17 different occasions during this period, while such proposals were debated in the full Senate on five occasions and twice in the House in these years. Electoral college-related amendments were approved by the necessary two-thirds majority twice in the Senate and once in the House, but never in the same Congress.[72]

For some years after that time, legislative interest in electoral college reform waned: no amendment to *reform* the electoral college has been introduced since the 107th Congress,[73] while no amendments to *replace* it with direct popular election were introduced between February 2011[74] and November 2016. Late in the 114th Congress, following the 2016 presidential election, four proposals to replace the electoral college with direct popular election were introduced,[75] but no action beyond committee referral was taken on them. Two resolutions proposing a constitutional amendment to establish direct popular vote have been introduced to date in the 115th Congress.[76]

---

[71] For additional information on reform proposals, please consult CRS Report R43824, *Electoral College Reform: Contemporary Issues for Congress*, by (name redacted).

[72] For a detailed examination and analysis of these efforts, please consult Peirce and Longley, *The People's President: The Electoral College in American History and the Direct Vote Alternative*, rev. ed. pp. 131-206.

[73] In the 107th Congress: H.J.Res. 1, 107th Congress, introduced by Rep. Clyburn, proposed a district system reform. H.J.Res. 17 and H.J.Res. 18, introduced by Rep. Engel, proposed a proportional system reform.

[74] In the 112th Congress, H.J.Res. 36, introduced by Rep. Jesse Jackson, Jr., proposed direct popular election.

[75] H.J.Res. 102, H.J.Res. 103, H.J.Res. 104, and S.J.Res. 41 in the 114th Congress.

[76] H.J.Res 19 and H.J.Res. 65.

Action at the State Level Since 2008

While Congress has not taken significant action on the question of electoral college reform in recent years, there has been considerable activity in the states.

Only an amendment can alter the constitutional structure of the electoral college, but the states retain considerable authority concerning various aspects of the system. For instance, as noted elsewhere in this report, Article II, Section 1, clause 2 gives the state legislature broad authority to "appoint" electors in any way they choose.

In practice, this appointment has been by popular election for 150 years. States also have authority over the formula by which electors are elected; as noted, 48 states and the District of Columbia use the general ticket system, but Maine and Nebraska adopted the district system or plan decades ago, an example of the states acting in their classic role as "laboratories of democracy."

In other words, the states are free to experiment with systems of elector selection and electoral vote allocation, up to a point. Over the past decade, both proportional and congressional district plan proposals have been advanced in the states, as identified in the following section, but none has been successful to date. These have included efforts in the following states:

- **California**—Ballot initiative campaigns in 2008 (the California Presidential Reform Act) and 2012 (the California Electoral College Reform Act) sought to establish a district system of electoral vote distribution and in 2014 (the California Split Electoral College Vote Distribution Initiative) to establish a proportional system by popular vote, but all three failed to gain ballot access.[77]

- **Colorado**—On November 2, 2004, Colorado voters rejected a state constitutional amendment, Amendment 36, which would have provided a rounded proportional allocation of electoral votes.[78] After a contentious campaign that gained a degree of national interest, the proposal was ultimately defeated by the voters.[79]

- **Michigan**—In 2011 and 2014, bills were introduced in the legislature to change electoral vote allocation in Michigan from the general ticket to the district system. No action beyond hearings was taken on either proposal.[80]

- **Nebraska**—Bills to return Nebraska from the district system to the general ticket allocation of electoral votes were introduced in the state's unicameral legislature

---

[77] 2008: please consult Shane Goldmacher, "Electoral College Measure Falls Short," *Sacramento Bee Capitol Alert*, February 5, 2008, available at http://blogs.sacbee.com/capitolalertlatest/2008/02/electoral-colle.html. 2012: "California Electoral College Reform Act," *Ballotpedia, an Interactive Almanac of U.S. Politics*, at http://ballotpedia.org/California_Electoral_College_Reform_Act_(2012). 2014: "California Split Electoral College Vote Distribution Initiative (2014), Ballotpedia, *an Interactive Almanac of U.S. Politics*, at http://ballotpedia.org/California_Split_Electoral_College_Vote_Distribution_Initiative_(2014).

[78] Amendment 36, available at http://www.lawanddemocracy.org/pdffiles/COamend36.pdf. Under the rounded proportional plan, percentages of the popular vote are rounded to whole numbers in determining the number of electoral votes awarded to competing candidates.

[79] Colorado, Secretary of State, *Official Publication of the Abstract of Votes Cast for the 2003 Coordinated[,] 2005 Primary[,] 2004 General [Elections]* (n.p., n.d.), pp. 138-139.

[80] Jonathan Oosting, "Michigan Panel Debates Presidential Election System, Electoral College Votes," *MLive.com*, September 25, 2015, at http://www.mlive.com/lansing-news/index.ssf/2015/09/michigan_2016_electoral_colleg.html

several times after 2011, most recently in 2016. None of these proposals has been successful to date.[81]

- **Pennsylvania**—In 2011 and 2012, two proposals were introduced in the Pennsylvania legislature to award the commonwealth's electoral votes according to the district system, but neither bill was enacted.[82] In 2013, legislation was introduced to award electoral votes according to the proportional system. As with earlier proposals, no action was taken beyond committee referral.[83]

- **Virginia**—In 2012, a variant of the district system was introduced in the Virginia General Assembly. In contrast to the system as enacted in Maine and Nebraska, which awards each state's two senatorial electors to the presidential ticket *winning the most popular votes statewide*, this legislation would have awarded the senatorial electors to the presidential ticket that won the popular vote *in the greatest number of congressional districts statewide*.[84] The bill was "bypassed indefinitely" in 2013.[85]

- **Wisconsin**—Between 2011 and 2014, press accounts indicated that Wisconsin state legislators would introduce legislation to award the state's electoral votes according to the district system. The Wisconsin Legislature's database for this period does not, however, identify any such proposal as having been introduced.[86]

Related activity in state legislatures continues following the 2016 presidential election. According to press reports, bills to change from the general ticket to district systems have been introduced in 2017 in the legislatures of Minnesota and Virginia.[87]

NGO Proposal: The National Popular Vote Initiative

Another contemporary effort centers on the National Popular Vote initiative, (NPV), a non-governmental campaign. NPV seeks to establish direct popular election of the President and Vice

---

[81] Martha Stoddard, "Bill to Return Nebraska to Winner-Take-All Electoral College Method Comes Up Short," *Omaha World Herald*, April 13, 2016, at http://www.omaha.com/news/legislature/bill-to-return-nebraska-to-winner-take-all-electoral-college/article_9c08b7c0-00be-11e6-b0fe-77966934ee98.html

[82] SB 1282, Regular Session, 2011-2012, Pennsylvania General Assembly website, at http://www.legis.state.pa.us/cfdocs/billinfo/billinfo.cfm?syear=2011&sind=0&body=S&type=B&BN=1282; HB 94, Regular Session, 2013-2014, Pennsylvania General Assembly website, at http://www.legis.state.pa.us/cfdocs/billinfo/bill_history.cfm?syear=2013&sind=0&body=H&type=B&bn=94.

[83] Senate Bill 538, Regular Session, 2013, Pennsylvania General Assembly website, at http://www.legis.state.pa.us/CFDOCS/Legis/PN/Public/btCheck.cfm?txtType=HTM&sessYr=2013&sessInd=0&billBody=S&billTyp=B&billNbr=0538&pn=0502

[84] Senate Bill SB 723, 2013 session, Virginia General Assembly, at http://lis.virginia.gov/cgi-bin/legp604.exe?131+sum+SB723.

[85] Senate Bill SB 723, 2013 session, Virginia General Assembly, at http://lis.virginia.gov/cgi-bin/legp604.exe?131+sum+SB723.

[86] Wisconsin Legislature, at https://docs.legis.wisconsin.gov/2015; https://docs.legis.wisconsin.gov/2013/; http://docs.legis.wisconsin.gov/2011.

[87] David Weigel, "Republicans in Virginia and Minnesota Propose Changes to Their Electoral College Rules," *Washington Post*, January 25, 2017, at https://www.washingtonpost.com/news/post-politics/wp/2017/01/25/republicans-in-minnesota-virginia-propose-changes-to-their-electoral-college-rules/?utm_term=.4370fb44dd49; "Proposals to Change Minnesota's Votes for President," Fox 9, January 26, 2017, at http://www.fox9.com/news/231915607-story.

President through an interstate compact, rather than by constitutional amendment.[88] Under the compact's provisions, the electoral college would remain, but the NPV members pledge to use their authority to appoint electors "in such manner as the Legislature thereof may direct" to choose in their states the ticket of electors committed to the candidates that gain *the most votes nationwide regardless of the popular vote results in their state*. Assuming all 50 states joined the NPV compact, this would arguably deliver a unanimous electoral college decision for the candidates winning the most popular votes.[89] The compact, however, would take effect only when states controlling a majority of the electoral college, that is, 270 or more electoral votes, approve the plan. Between 2007 and 2014, 10 states and the District of Columbia joined the compact. They are allocated a total of 165 electoral votes, 61% of the 270 vote majority that would be required for the compact to be implemented.[90] According to National Popular Vote, Inc., the national advocacy group for the NPV initiative, the compact has been introduced in all 50 states and the District of Columbia, and in 2017 was under active consideration in the legislatures of 18 states that control 225 electoral votes.[91]

Concluding Observations

The electoral college system has demonstrated both durability and adaptability during more than two centuries of government under the U.S. Constitution. Although its constitutional elements have remained largely unchanged since ratification of the Twelfth Amendment, the electoral college has never worked as the founders planned. The historical record reveals that they intended it to be an indirect, deliberative selection process, carefully filtered from political considerations, with the degree of voter participation left to the discretion of the state legislatures. Instead, it accommodated the demands of an increasingly democratic and political party-dominated presidential election system, ultimately evolving into an improvised yet enduring assemblage of constitutional provisions, state laws, political party practices, and traditions.

The Constitution sets the size of the electoral college, the allocation of electors among the states, the margin of votes needed to win, and procedures for contingent election. Federal law establishes the quadrennial schedule that prescribes the times when presidential elections are held, and when electoral votes are cast in the states and then counted and recorded in Congress. It also sets federal procedures for each of these stages in the election process. State law provides who shall vote for electors, how elector-candidates shall be nominated, how electoral votes shall be awarded, and, in some states, seeks to prohibit or discourage faithless electors.

---

[88] For more detailed information and analysis of the National Popular Vote Initiative, including relevant political, legal, and constitutional issues, please consult CRS Report R43823, *The National Popular Vote Initiative: Direct Election of the President by Interstate Compact*, by (name redacted) and (name redacted).

[89] Even under NPV, however, the potential for faithless electors who vote against instructions would remain.

[90] "61% of the Way to Activating the National Popular Vote Bill," National Popular Vote website, at http://www.nationalpopularvote.com/status. The following states are current signatories of the National Popular Vote Interstate Compact. They are listed in chronological order of their accession, including electoral vote totals, Hawaii (4), 2008; Illinois (20), 2008; Maryland (10), 2008; New Jersey (14), 2008; Washington (12), 2009; Massachusetts (11), 2010; District of Columbia (3), 2010; Vermont (3), 2011; California (55), 2011; Rhode Island (4), 2013; and New York (29), 2014.

[91] In 2017, The NPV Interstate Compact is currently under consideration in the legislatures of following states, which are allocated a total of 225 electoral votes. They are listed in alphabetical order, including electoral vote totals: Alaska (3), Arizona (11), Connecticut (7), Florida (29), Georgia (16), Idaho (4), Indiana (11), Kansas (6), Minnesota (10), Missouri (10), Nevada (6), New Mexico (5), North Carolina (15), Ohio (18), Oregon (7), Pennsylvania (20), South Carolina (9), and Texas (38), National Popular Vote website, at http://www.nationalpopularvote.com/state-status and state legislative websites.

While this arrangement may not work as the founders intended, its defenders would note the electoral college system has elected the presidential candidate who arguably enjoyed the greatest public support in 53 of 58 elections under the Constitution—a "success rate" of 91.4%. At the same time, opponents could note the 2016 contest, in which a President was elected with an electoral college majority, but fewer votes than his principal opponent. To this they might add the election was also characterized by the largest number of faithless electors in recent history. The 2016 election has contributed to renewed interest in reform proposals in Congress, particularly direct popular election, but the prospects for legislative action remain uncertain.

Notwithstanding the results of the 2016 presidential contest, however, electoral college reform does not appear to be an urgent public issue at present.

Given the stringent requirements faced by all proposed constitutional amendments, changing opinion of the electoral college system among Republican poll respondents, the slow progress of the National Popular Vote Initiative, and particularly the failure of the reform issue to command the substantial congressional support and attention, the electoral college system seems likely to remain in place unless or until its alleged failings become so compelling that a broad consensus in favor of reform or abolition emerges among the public and in Congress and the states.

Counting Electoral Votes: An Overview of Procedures at the Joint Session, Including Objections by Members of Congress

November 15, 2016

RL32717

The Constitution and federal law establish a detailed timetable following the presidential election during which time the members of the electoral college convene in the 50 state capitals and in the District of Columbia, cast their votes for President and Vice President, and submit their votes through state officials to both houses of Congress. The electoral votes are scheduled to be opened before a joint session of Congress on January 6, 2017. Federal law specifies the procedures which are to be followed at this session and provides procedures for challenges to the validity of an electoral vote. This report describes the steps in the process and precedents set in prior presidential elections governing the actions of the House and Senate in certifying the electoral vote and in responding to challenges of the validity of one or more electoral votes from one or more states.

This report has been revised, and will be updated on a periodic basis to provide the dates for the relevant joint session of Congress, and to reflect any new, relevant precedents or practices.

From Election to Inauguration—An Overview of the Process

The House and Senate are scheduled to convene in joint session on January 6, 2017, for the purpose of opening the 2016 presidential election electoral votes submitted by state government officials, certifying their validity, counting them, and declaring the official result of the election for President and Vice President.[1] This report describes the steps which precede the joint session and the procedures set in the Constitution and statute by which the House and Senate jointly certify the results of the electoral vote. It also discusses the procedures set in law governing challenges to the validity of an electoral vote, and makes reference to the procedures followed during the joint session in 2005 by which the election of George W. Bush was certified.

Much of what follows in this report is based on the United States Constitution (particularly Article II, Section 1, and Amendment 12), and on a federal law enacted in 1887 (the Electoral Count Act of 1887) and amended in 1948, now codified in Title 3 of the *United States Code*.[2] Reference is also made to congressional precedent and practice. Early congressional precedents on the counting of electoral votes, which may be found in *Hinds' and Cannon's Precedents of the House of Representatives*, are sometimes inconsistent with each other and with more recent practice. This record, coupled with disputes over the electoral count in 1877, provided the impetus for codifying procedure in the 1887 law. Precedents which pre-date the 1887 act may be primarily of historical significance, particularly to the extent that they are inconsistent with express provisions of the 1887 act, as amended.

Due to the absence of specific and persuasive authority on some issues, and in the interest of brevity, this report attempts to at least identify and present some of the possible issues and questions that have been raised, even when not necessarily resolving them by reference to authoritative source material or decisions. The topics presented are arranged in the approximate order of their occurrence.

Actions Leading Up to the Joint Session

Appointment of Electors: Election Day

The United States Constitution provides that each state "shall appoint" electors for President and Vice President in the manner directed by its state legislature (Article II, Section 1, clause 2), on the day which may be determined by Congress (Article II, Section 1, clause 3). Congress has determined in federal law that the "electors of President and Vice President shall be appointed, in each State" on Election Day, that is, the "Tuesday next after the first Monday in November" every fourth year (on November 8, 2016) (3 U.S.C. §1).

Final State Determination of Election Contests and Controversies

Congress has, since 1887, sought to place the responsibility for resolving election contests and challenges to presidential elections in a state upon the state itself. Federal law provides that if a state, under its established statutory procedure, has made a "final determination of any controversy or contest" relative to the presidential election in the state, and if that determination is

---

[1] The permanent statutory date for the joint session of Congress to count the electoral votes is January 6 of the year immediately after the meeting of the electors (3 U.S.C. §15). This date can be changed by Congress by law. See, e.g., P.L. 112-228, H.J.Res. 122, 112th Congress (2011-2012), when January 6 was to fall on a Sunday.

[2] 3 U.S.C. §§3-21. See 24 Stat. 373, ch. 90, 49th Cong., February 3, 1887; 62 Stat. 671, P.L. 771, June 25, 1948, enacting Title 3, United States Code, into positive law.

completed under this procedure at least six days before the electors are to meet to vote, such determination is to be considered "conclusive" as to which electors were appointed on election day (3 U.S.C. §5).[3] As explained below, the electors vote on December 19, 2016, so the last day for making a final determination is December 13, 2016.

Certification by the Governor

The governor of each state is required by federal law "as soon as practicable" after the "final ascertainment" of the appointment of the electors, or "as soon as practicable" after the "final determination of any controversy or contest" concerning such election under its statutory procedure for election contests, to send to the Archivist of the United States by registered mail and under state seal, "a certificate of such ascertainment of the electors appointed," including the names and numbers of votes for each person for whose appointment as elector any votes were given (3 U.S.C. §6).

Duplicate Certificates to Electors

On or before December 19, 2016, the governor of each state is required to deliver to the electors of the state six duplicate-originals of the certificate sent to the Archivist of the United States under state seal (3 U.S.C. §6).

Meetings of Electors to Cast Votes

The electors of each state meet at the place designated by that state, on the first Monday after the second Wednesday in December (December 19, 2016), to cast their votes for President and Vice President of the United States (United States Constitution, Amendment 12; 3 U.S.C. §§7,8).

Electors' Certifications of Votes

After the electors have voted in each state, they make and sign six certificates of their votes containing two distinct lists, one being the votes for President and the other the votes for Vice President. The law instructs the electors to attach to these lists a certificate furnished to them by the governor; to seal those certificates and to certify on them that these are all of the votes for President and Vice President; and then to send one certificate to the President of the Senate, and two certificates to the secretary of state of their state (one to be held subject to the order of the President of the Senate). On the day after their meeting (December 20, 2016), the electors are to forward by registered mail two of the certificates to the Archivist of the United States (one to be held subject to the order of the President of the Senate), and one to the federal judge in the district where the electors have assembled (3 U.S.C. §§9,10,11).

Congressional Demand for Certificates

If no certificates of votes or lists have been received by the President of the Senate or the Archivist from electors by the fourth Wednesday in December (December 28, 2016), then the President of the Senate (or the Archivist if the President of the Senate is not available) is directed by law to request the state's secretary of state to immediately forward the certificates and lists

---

[3] The six-day period established in law has been referred to as the "Safe Harbor" requirement, in that electoral vote results certified by that date are considered to be conclusively cast. See, e.g., *Bush v. Gore,* 531 U.S. 98, 110-11 (2000).

lodged with the secretary of state, and to send a special messenger to the local federal district judge to transmit the lists that are to be lodged with that judge (3 U.S.C. §§12,13).

Archivist's Transmittal of Certificates to Congress

At the first meeting of Congress, set for January 3, 2017, the Archivist of the United States is required to transmit to the two houses every certificate received from the governors of the states (3 U.S.C. §6).

Date for Counting Electoral Votes

The date for counting the electoral votes is fixed by law as January 6 following each presidential election (3 U.S.C. §15), unless the date is changed by law. For example, when January 6, 2013, was to fall on a Sunday, the date was changed to January 4, 2013, when the President signed H.J.Res. 122 on December 28, 2012.

Providing for the Joint Session

Venue for Counting Electoral Votes

The electoral votes are counted at a joint session of the Senate and the House of Representatives, meeting in the House chamber. (The *United States Code* refers to the event as a joint meeting; it also has been characterized in the *Congressional Record* as a joint convention.) The joint session convenes at 1:00 p.m. on that day. The President of the Senate is the presiding officer (3 U.S.C. §15). The President pro tempore of the Senate has presided in the absence of the President of the Senate.[4]

Opening of the Votes

Under 3 U.S.C. §15, the President of the Senate opens and presents the certificates of the electoral votes of the states and the District of Columbia in alphabetical order. (As discussed above, under 3 U.S.C. §§9-10, the electors in each state, having voted, are to sign, seal, and certify the certificates. Under §11 of the same title, they are to mail one such certificate to the President of the Senate and mail two others to the Archivist of the United States.)

Reading of the Votes by House and Senate Tellers

The certificate, or an equivalent document, from each state and the District of Columbia then is to be read by tellers previously appointed from among the membership of the House and Senate. Before the joint session convenes, each chamber appoints two of its Members to be the tellers (the appointments are made by the presiding officers of the respective chambers, based on recommendations made to them by the leaders of the two major parties). The appointed tellers are often members of the House Administration and Senate Rules and Administration Committees, the panels in each chamber having jurisdiction over matters relating to the election of the President and Vice President. In 2013, the House tellers were Members who would serve as chair

---

[4] In January, 1969, Vice President Humphrey "declined to preside over the joint session to count the electoral votes." *Deschler's [and Deschler-Brown] Precedents of the United States House of Representatives,* 94th Cong., 2nd sess., H.Doc. 94-661 (Washington: GPO, 1977) [hereafter *Deschler's Precedents*], ch. 10, §2.5, p. 10.

and ranking member of the House Administration Committee that Congress. The Senate tellers were the chair and ranking member of the Senate Rules and Administration Committee.[5]

Counting the Votes and Announcing the Result

After the votes of each state and the District of Columbia have been read, the tellers record and count them. When this process has been completed, the presiding officer announces whether any candidates have received the required majority votes for President and Vice President. If so, that "announcement shall be deemed a sufficient declaration of the persons, if any, elected President and Vice President of the United States" (3 U.S.C. §15).

Expediting the Process of Opening and Reading Votes

The joint session may agree to expedite this process when no controversy is anticipated. In the 1997 joint meeting, for example, the Vice President announced: "Under well-established precedents, unless a motion shall be made in any case, the reading of the formal portions of the certificates will be dispensed with. After ascertainment has been had that the certificates are authentic and correct in form, the tellers will count and make a list of the votes cast by the electors of the several States."[6] The Vice President proceeded to open the certificates in alphabetical order and passed to the tellers the certificates showing the votes of the electors in each state and the District of Columbia. In each case, the tellers then read, counted, and announced the result for each state and the District of Columbia. According to the *Congressional Record*, the joint session consumed precisely 24 minutes. A similar process was followed in 2013, when, according to the *Congressional Record*, the joint session consumed 23 minutes.[7]

The Majority Required for Election

The 12th Amendment requires the winning candidate to receive "a majority of the whole number of Electors appointed." That number normally becomes the same as a majority of the number of electoral votes counted by the tellers.

One exception that has been identified occurred in 1873 when the Vice President announced that President Ulysses S. Grant had received "a majority of the whole number of electoral votes," even though he also indicated that not all of those electoral votes had been counted. In that case, the two houses, under procedures similar to those described below, had decided not to count the electoral votes from Arkansas and Louisiana. Nonetheless, the number of electoral votes allocated to Arkansas and Louisiana evidently were included in "the whole number of electoral votes" for purposes of determining whether President Grant had received the majority required for election.[8] It should be noted that President Grant was victorious by whichever standard was used. He

---

[5] In 2009, the Senate tellers initially were the chair and ranking member of the Senate Rules and Administration Committee, but another Senator, who would become chair of the Rules and Administration Committee that Congress, was later appointed in lieu of the Senator who had served as chair in the previous Congress. On the first day of the 111th Congress, the Vice President appointed Senator Dianne Feinstein of California and Senator Robert Bennett of Utah to serve as tellers to count the electoral votes (*Congressional Record*, daily edition, vol. 155 [January 6, 2009], p. S7). On January 8, 2009, the Senate agreed by unanimous consent that Senator Charles Schumer of New York would serve as a teller in lieu of Senator Feinstein (*Congressional Record*, daily edition, vol. 155 [January 8, 2009], p. S186).

[6] *Congressional Record*, vol. 143 (January 9, 1997), p. 297.

[7] *Congressional Record*, vol. 159 (January 4, 2013), p. H49.

[8] *Congressional Globe*, vol. 46 (February 12, 1873), pp. 1305-1306.

received 286 electoral votes out of the 352 electoral votes counted, or out of the potential 364 electoral votes (if the contested votes from Arkansas and Louisiana were included in the whole number).

In 1865, by contrast, only two of the three Nevada electors cast their electoral votes. In the joint session, only two Nevada votes were counted and included in the "whole number of electoral votes."[9] Similar instances of votes "not given" by electors not being included in the "whole number" of electors reported, thus reducing the so-called denominator and the "majority" needed to elect, occurred in 1809, 1813, and 1817.[10]

We are not aware of instances in which this issue has become a source of contention or was determinative of which candidate was elected. If electoral votes from a state or the District of Columbia were not available to be counted during the joint session (and if the question were raised in a timely fashion), the joint session might be called upon to address the effect of this situation on what number of votes would constitute the "majority of the whole number of Electors appointed."

Procedures for Conducting the Joint Session

Title 3 of the U.S. Code includes provisions governing the conduct of the joint session. Section 16 of Title 3 is intended to ensure that the joint session conducts and completes its business expeditiously. As discussed below, §18 prohibits debate as well as the offering and consideration of almost all questions. Section 16 provides that the joint session is to continue until the count is completed and the result announced, and limits recesses if the process of counting the votes and announcing the results becomes time-consuming. The seating of Senators, Representatives, and officials (the Clerk of the House, the Secretary of the Senate, the Members designated as tellers, and other administrative officers of the House and Senate) is also governed by §16.

Under §18, the President of the Senate is to preserve order. This authority *may* be interpreted as encompassing the authority to decide questions of order, but the statute is not explicit on this point. Nevertheless, on several occasions during the joint session of January 6, 2001, Vice President Albert A. Gore, Jr., presiding over the joint session, ruled on the admissibility of objections to the receipt of electoral votes from the state of Florida, and also advised House and Senate Members that debate was not permitted and that a unanimous consent request for debate on the issue could not be entertained. He further stated that even incidental parliamentary motions, including those that only affect the actions of the House, needed the written endorsement of at least one Representative and one Senator in order to be valid. Vice President Gore also declined to entertain a point of order that no quorum was present because the point of order had not been endorsed by one Member from each chamber.[11] The statute provides that no question is to be "put by the presiding officer except to either House on a motion to withdraw." (The statute provides for the Senate to withdraw automatically under circumstances discussed below. The statute, however, makes no other explicit reference to a *motion* to withdraw.)

---

[9] *Congressional Globe,* vol. 35, February 8, 1865, pp. 668-669.

[10] See CRS Report RL30769, *Electoral Vote Counts in Congress: Survey of Certain Congressional Practices,* by (name redacted) et al.

[11] For the full transcript of the joint session of January 6, 2001, see *Congressional Record,* vol. 147 (January 6, 2001), pp. 101-115.

Objecting to the Counting of One or More Electoral Votes

Provisions in 3 U.S.C. §15 include a procedure for making and acting on objections to the counting of one or more of the electoral votes from a state or the District of Columbia. When the certificate or equivalent paper from each state (or the District of Columbia) is read, "the President of the Senate shall call for objections, if any." Any such objection must be presented in writing and must be signed by at least one Senator and one Representative. The objection "shall state clearly and concisely, and without argument, the ground thereof.... " During the joint session of January 6, 2001, the presiding officer intervened on several occasions to halt attempts to make speeches under the guise of offering an objection.

When an objection, properly made in writing and endorsed by at least one Senator and one Representative, is received, each house is to meet and consider it separately. The statute states that "[n]o votes or papers from any other State shall be acted upon until the objections previously made to the votes or papers from any State shall have been finally disposed of." However, in 1873, before enactment of the law now in force, the joint session agreed, without objection and for reasons of convenience, to entertain objections with regard to two or more states before the houses met separately on any of them.

Disposing of Objections

The joint session does not act on any objections that are made. Instead, the joint session is suspended while each house meets separately to debate the objection and vote whether, based on the objection, to count the vote or votes in question. Both houses must vote separately to agree to the objection. Otherwise, the objection fails and the vote or votes are counted. (3 U.S.C. §15, provides that "the two Houses concurrently may reject the vote or votes.... ")

These procedures have been invoked twice since enactment of the 1887 law. The first was an instance of what has been called the "faithless elector" problem. In 1969, a Representative (James O'Hara of Michigan) and a Senator (Edmund S. Muskie of Maine) objected in writing to counting the vote of an elector from North Carolina who had been expected to cast his vote for Richard Nixon and Spiro Agnew, but who instead cast his vote for George Wallace and Curtis LeMay. Both chambers met and voted separately to reject the objection, so when the joint session resumed, the challenged electoral vote was counted as cast.[12] In that instance, the elector whose vote was challenged was from a state that did not by law "bind" its electors to vote only for the candidates to whom they were pledged. The instance of a "faithless" elector from a state that does, in fact, bind the elector by law to vote for the candidate to whom listed or pledged has not yet been expressly addressed by Congress or the courts.[13]

---

[12] When the two chambers reconvened in joint session, the Secretary of the Senate reported that the Senate had agreed to the following action: "Ordered, that the Senate by a vote of 33 ayes to 58 nays rejects the objection to the electoral votes cast in the State of North Carolina for George C. Wallace for President and Curtis E. LeMay for Vice President." The Clerk of the House stated the results of the House action: "Ordered, that the House of Representatives rejects the objection to the electoral vote of the State of North Carolina submitted by the Representative from Michigan, Mr. O'Hara, and the Senator from Maine, Mr. Muskie." *Congressional Record*, vol. 115 (January 6, 1969), p. 171. The House vote was 170-228. See also *Deschler's Precedents*, vol. 3, chap. 10, §3.6. Both houses used roll call votes to decide the question.

[13] See *Ray v. Blair*, 343 U.S. 214 (1952) in which the Court upheld the permissibility of such state limitations but did not address their enforceability.

The second instance was related to reported voting irregularities in Ohio. In 2005, a Representative (Stephanie Tubbs Jones of Ohio) and a Senator (Barbara Boxer of California) objected in writing to the Ohio electoral votes. The chambers withdrew from the joint session to consider the objection, and the House and Senate each rejected the objection. When the House and Senate resumed the joint session, the electoral votes were counted as cast.[14]

Procedures for Considering Objections

3 U.S.C. §17 lays out procedures for each house to follow in debating and voting on an objection. These procedures limit debate on the objection to not more than two hours, during which each Member may speak only once, and for not more than five minutes. Then "it shall be the duty of the presiding officer of each House to put the main question without further debate." Under this provision, the presiding officer in each house held in 1969 that a motion to table the objection was not in order.[15]

In the House, the Speaker announced both in 1969 and 2005 that he would attempt to recognize supporters of the objection and opponents in an alternating fashion for the duration of the two-hour period. In one instance in 1969, the Speaker inquired whether a Member supported or opposed the challenge before he agreed to recognize him to speak. Members can yield to each other during debate as they can during five-minute debate in the Committee of the Whole, and many chose to do so in 2005. The Speaker also entertained unanimous consent requests to insert material in the *Congressional Record*.

In 1969 the Senate agreed, by unanimous consent, to a different way in which the time for debate was to be controlled and allocated, granting one hour each to the majority and minority leaders and authorizing them to yield not more than five minutes to any Senator seeking recognition to speak.[16] The five-minute debate prescribed in the statute was followed in 2005, however, and the Presiding Officer entertained requests to insert statements into the *Congressional Record*.

Basis for Objections

The general grounds for an objection to the counting of an electoral vote or votes would appear from the federal statute and from historical sources to be that such vote was not "regularly given" by an elector, and/or that the elector was not "lawfully certified" according to state statutory procedures. The statutory provision first provides in the negative that "no electoral vote ... regularly given by electors whose appointment has been lawfully certified ... from which but one return has been received shall be rejected" (3 U.S.C. §15), and then reiterates for clarity[17] that both houses concurrently may reject a vote when not "so regularly given" by electors "so certified" (3 U.S.C. §15). It should be noted that the word "lawfully" was expressly inserted by the House in the Senate legislation (S. 9, 49th Congress) before the word "certified."[18] Such

---

[14] When the two chambers reconvened in joint session, the Secretary of the Senate reported that the Senate had agreed to the following action: "Ordered, that the Senate by a vote of 1 aye to 74 nays rejects the objection to the electoral votes cast in the State of Ohio for George W. Bush for President and Richard Cheney for Vice President." The Clerk of the House then stated the results of the House action: "Ordered, that the House of Representatives rejects the objection to the electoral vote of the State of Ohio." *Congressional Record*, daily edition, vol. 151 (January 6, 2005), p. H128. The House vote was 31-267. Both houses used roll call votes to decide the question.

[15] *Deschler's Precedents*, ch. 10, §3.7, pp. 18-20.

[16] *Deschler's Precedents*, ch. 10, §3.8, pp. 20-23.

[17] See Conference Report on 1887 legislation, *Congressional Record*, vol. 18 (January 14, 1887), p. 668.

[18] Ibid.

addition arguably provides an indication that Congress thought it might, as grounds for an objection, question and look into the lawfulness of the certification under state law. The objection that votes were not "regularly given" may, in practice, subsume the objection that the elector was not "lawfully certified," for a vote given by one not "lawfully certified" may arguably be other than "regularly given." Nevertheless, the two objections are not necessarily the same. In the case of the so-called "faithless elector" in 1969, described above, the elector was apparently "lawfully certified" by the state, but the objection raised was that the vote was not "regularly given" by such elector. In the above-described 2005 case, the objection was also based on the grounds that the electoral votes "were not, under all of the known circumstances, regularly given."

Receipt of Two Certificates from the Same State

Influenced by its historical experience prior to 1887, Congress was particularly concerned in the statute of 1887 with the case of two lists of electors and votes being presented to Congress from the same state. Three different contingencies appear to be provided for in the statute for two lists being presented. In the first instance, two lists would be proffered, but the assumption presented in the law is that only one list would be from electors who were determined to be appointed pursuant to the state election contest statute (as provided for in 3 U.S.C. §5), and that in such case, only those electors should be counted. In the second case, when two lists were proffered as being from two *different* state authorities who arguably made determinations provided for under 3 U.S.C. §5 (a state statutory election contest determined at least six days prior to December 18, the winner of the state presidential election), the question of which state authority is "the lawful tribunal of such State" to make the decision (and thus the acceptance of those electors' votes) shall be decided only upon the concurrent agreement of *both* houses "supported by the decision of such State so authorized by its law...." In the third instance, if there is *no* determination by a state authority of the question of which slate was lawfully appointed, then the two chambers must agree concurrently to accept the votes of one set of electors; but the two chambers may also concurrently agree not to accept the votes of electors from that state.

When the two houses disagree, then the statute states that the votes of the electors whose appointment was certified by the governor of the state shall be counted. It is not precisely clear whether this provision for resolving cases in which the House and Senate vote differently applies only to the last two situations (that is, when either *two* determinations have allegedly been made under state contest law and procedure, or *no* such determination has been made); or, instead, also when only one such determination is present. Although this section of the statute is not free from doubt, its structure and its relationship to §5 (and to give effect to §5) seem to indicate that when there is only *one* determination by the state made in a *timely* fashion under the state's election contest law and procedures (even when there are two or more lists or slates of electors presented before Congress), then Congress shall accept that state determination (3 U.S.C. §15) as "conclusive" (3 U.S.C. §5). By this interpretation, the language providing that if the House and Senate split, the question shall be decided in favor of the choice certified by the governor, may not have been intended to be applicable to cases covered by the first clause in the statute in which only one slate or group has been determined, in a timely fashion, to be the electors through the state's procedures for election contests and controversies. *Hinds' Precedents of the House of Representatives* suggests that when a state has settled the matter "in accordance with a law of that state six days before the time for the meeting of electors," then a controversy over the appointment of electors in that state "shall not be a cause of question in the counting of the electoral vote by Congress."[19] It should be noted that *Hinds'* cites no precedent or ruling, but

---

[19] Asher C. Hinds, *Hinds' Precedents of the House of Representatives of the United States* (Washington: GPO, 1907- (continued...)

merely paraphrases the statute, and it seems likely that this issue of the lawfulness of the determination and certification by a state could be raised and dealt with in the joint session.

Precedent subsequent to the statute's original enactment in 1887 has been sparse. There appears only to have been one example, in 1961, when the governor of the state of Hawaii first certified the electors of Vice President Richard M. Nixon as having been appointed, and then, due to a subsequent recount which determined that Senator John F. Kennedy had won the Hawaii vote, certified Senator Kennedy as the winner. Both slates of electors had met on the prescribed day in December, cast their votes for President and Vice President, and transmitted them according to the federal statute. This was the case even though the recount was apparently not completed until a later date, that is, not until December 28.[20] The presiding officer, that is, the President of the Senate, Vice President Nixon, suggested "without the intent of establishing a precedent" that the latter and more recent certification of Senator Kennedy be accepted so as "not to delay the further count of electoral votes." This was agreed to by unanimous consent.[21]

Electoral Vote Timetable and Subsequent Action

The timetable for the certification, transmission, review, and approval of the electoral votes was established by Congress to avoid a repetition of the extraordinary delay incident to the electoral vote controversy surrounding the 1876 presidential election. In the event that no candidate has received a majority of the electoral vote for President, the election is ultimately to be decided by the House of Representatives in which the names of the three candidates receiving the most electoral votes for President are considered by the House, with each state having one vote. In the event that no candidate receives a majority of the electoral votes for Vice President, the names of the two candidates receiving the highest number of electoral votes for that post are submitted to the Senate, which elects the Vice President by majority vote of the Senators. The development and current practices for election of the President and Vice President by Congress specified in the Constitution and law are discussed in detail in CRS Report RL32695, *Election of the President and Vice President by Congress: Contingent Election*, by (name redacted) .

(...continued)
1908), vol. 3, §1914, p. 202, referring only to the 1887 statute).
[20] *Facts on File, Weekly World News Digest*, vol. XX, no. 1052, December 22-28, 1960, p. 469.
[21] See discussion in *Deschler's Precedents*, ch. 10, §3.5, pp. 12-13.

Presidential Transitions: Issues Involving Outgoing and Incoming Administrations

May 17, 2017

RL34722

The smooth and orderly transfer of power generally is a notable feature of presidential transitions, and a testament to the legitimacy and durability of the electoral and democratic processes. Yet, at the same time, a variety of events, decisions, and activities contribute to what some may characterize as the unfolding drama of a presidential transition. Interparty transitions in particular might be contentious. Using the various powers available, a sitting President might use the transition period to attempt to secure his legacy or effect policy changes. Some observers have suggested that, if the incumbent has lost the election, he might try to enact policies in the waning months of his presidency that would "tie his successor's hands." On the other hand, a President-elect, once in office, and eager to establish his policy agenda and populate his Administration with his appointees, will be involved in a host of decisions and activities, some of which might modify or overturn the previous Administration's actions or decisions.

The President's authority to exercise power begins immediately upon being sworn into office and continues until he is no longer the officeholder. By the same token, while congressional oversight of the executive branch is continuous, some activities may take on special significance at the end or beginning of an Administration. The disposition of government records (including presidential records and vice presidential records), protections against "burrowing in" (which involves the conversion of political appointees to career status in the civil service), the granting of pardons, and the issuance of "midnight rules" are four activities associated largely with the outgoing President's Administration. The incumbent President may also submit a budget to Congress, or he may defer to his successor on this matter. Continuing this transition process, the first actions of a new President generally focus on establishing the priorities and leadership of the Administration. These can include executive orders, appointments to positions that require Senate confirmation as well as those that do not, and efforts to influence the pace and substance of agency rulemaking.

Depending upon the particular activity or function, the extent and type of Congress's involvement in presidential transitions may vary. As an example of direct involvement, the Senate confirms the President's appointees to certain positions. On the other hand, Congress is not involved in the issuance of executive orders, but it may exercise oversight, or take some other action regarding the Administration's activities.

Introduction

At its heart, a presidential transition is the transfer of executive power from the incumbent President to his or her successor. A single step—taking the oath of the office of President—accomplishes this transfer. However, a successful transition between the incumbent Administration and the incoming Administration begins with pre-election planning and continues through inauguration day. It involves key personnel from the outgoing and incoming Presidents' staffs, requires resources, and includes a host of activities, such as vetting candidates for positions in the new Administration, helping to familiarize the incoming Administration with the operations of the executive branch, and developing a comprehensive policy platform. The importance of a well-organized, coherent transition has been underscored by the ongoing security concerns following the terrorist attacks of September 11, 2001. In 2015, the Senate Committee on Homeland Security and Governmental Affairs (HSGAC) acknowledged the importance of presidential transition planning in "prevent[ing] disruptions that can create vulnerabilities to the nation's security," adding that "[t]he challenges and risks identified by the Committee have only increased since 2010."[1]

Over the years, presidential administrations' commitment to and involvement in transition activities have varied. As the Partnership for Public Service has noted

> For much of American history, presidential transitions were carried out without very much advance planning or even cooperation from the sitting chief executive. A president-elect was not expected to come to the nation's capital until the inauguration and had few if any substantial policy or procedural discussions with the outgoing administration.[2]

Additionally, presidential candidates generally have eschewed pre-election planning. Their reluctance to begin transition activities prior the general election appears to stem from, at least in part, a concern that the appearance of presuming victory could lead to criticism or possibly even a backlash at the polls. Other possible reasons why they might defer transition activities until after the election include concerns that such activities "could tax limited resources, [or] distract or conflict key campaign staff...."[3]

Growing recognition of the necessity of a well-planned, organized, and coordinated transition to a new Administration's ability to assume responsibility on inauguration day for governing has shifted stakeholders' perspectives. Contributing to the impetus for a more robust transition with a longer lead time (i.e., pre-election planning) was the realization that the period of time between the date of the general election and inauguration day is insufficient for accomplishing necessary tasks and activities given the complexity of a presidential transition and the federal government. In its report on legislation that subsequently was enacted as P.L. 111-283, Pre-Election Presidential Transition Act of 2010, HSGAC wrote: "By codifying Congress's view that candidates should start transition planning before the election, this legislation seeks to remove the

---

[1] U.S. Congress, Senate Committee on Homeland Security and Governmental Affairs, *Presidential Transitions Improvements Act of 2015*, report to accompany S. 1172, 114th Cong., 1st sess., July 27, 2015, S.Rept. 114-94 (Washington: GPO, 2015), pp. 2-3.

[2] Partnership for Public Service, *Ready to Govern: Improving the Presidential Transition*, January 2010, p. 1.

[3] U.S. Congress, Senate Homeland Security and Governmental Affairs Committee, *Pre-Election Presidential Transition Act of 2010*, report to accompany S. 3106, 111th Cong., 2nd sess., August 2, 2010, S.Rept. 111-239 (Washington: GPO, 2010), p. 3.

stigma related to it and make pre-election transition planning an accepted part of a successful transition process."[4]

Establishing a Presidential Transition Framework

The passage and implementation of the Presidential Transition Act (PTA) of 1963 and subsequent amendments led to the provision of services and facilities to transition teams and the establishment of formal mechanisms to facilitate presidential transitions while legitimizing pre-election planning by candidates.[5] Under this statute, the Administration is authorized to provide pre-election transition support to eligible candidates, required to establish a White House Transition Coordinating Council and an Agency Transition Directors Council, and authorized to provide transition-related facilities and services to the incoming Administration. This commitment of resources on the part of the federal government (particularly the White House), as well as on the part of the presidential candidates, and, ultimately, the President-elect, highlights the importance of the presidential transition to the continuity of operations of the federal government. A successful transition facilitates the formation of a new Administration, familiarizes top-level personnel (who may not have prior public service experience) with the operations of the federal government generally or particular agencies, and prepares the incoming Administration to govern.

Governing presents its own challenges to a new Administration. The Partnership for Public Service notes that an incoming President "is responsible for making more than 4,000 appointments and managing an organization with a budget of nearly $4 trillion and more than 2 million civilian employees performing missions as diverse as national defense, securing our borders, conducting medical research and reducing homelessness."[6] The number of federal agencies and the variety of their missions serve as a proxy for the complexity of the federal government. The 15 executive departments alone are responsible for a broad range of missions, policies, functions, and programs, yet they represent a small percentage of the hundreds of federal government entities.[7] As suggested above, reviewing the staffing needs of a new Administration provides another perspective on the complexity of the federal government. Bradley Patterson estimated that, in 2008, 7,854 positions were to be filled by the President and the White House staff.[8] This figure included 1,756 presidential appointees requiring Senate confirmation, 2,530 presidential appointees that did not require Senate confirmation, 400 federal judicial appointees,

---

[4] Ibid.

[5] P.L. 88-277, Presidential Transition Act of 1963; P.L. 100-398, Presidential Transition Effectiveness Act of 1988; P.L. 106-293, Presidential Transition Act of 2000; Section 7601 of P.L. 108-458, Intelligence Reform and Terrorism Prevent Act (IRTPA) of 2004; P.L. 111-283, Pre-Election Presidential Transition Act of 2010; and P.L. 114-136, Edward "Ted" Kaufman and Michael Leavitt Presidential Transitions Improvements Act of 2015. The Presidential Transition Act of 1963, as amended, may be found in 3 U.S.C. §102 note. For information regarding the Presidential Transition Act, as amended, see CRS Report RS22979, *Presidential Transition Act: Provisions and Funding*, by (name redacted).

[6] Center for Presidential Transition, Partnership for Public Service, *Presidential Transition Guide*, April 2016, 2nd ed., p. 10.

[7] The executive departments are Agriculture, Commerce, Defense, Education, Energy, Health and Human Services, Homeland Security, Housing and Urban Development, Interior, Justice, Labor, State, Transportation, Treasury, and Veterans Affairs. See https://www.usa.gov/federal-agencies/a for a list of federal government organizations.

[8] Martha Joynt Kumar, *Before the Oath: How George W. Bush and Barack Obama Managed a Transfer of Power* (Baltimore: Johns Hopkins University Press, 2015), p. 19.

944 White House staff positions, and 2,224 noncareer Senior Executive Service and Schedule C positions.[9]

Presidential Transitions and National Security

In light of the terrorist attacks of September 11, 2001, recent terrorist incidents in the United States and abroad, and the threat of a terrorist attack on the 2009 inauguration, an overarching issue for presidential transitions is national security. During the hours leading up to the January 20, 2009, inauguration of Barack Obama, the Federal Bureau of Investigation (FBI) briefed senior officials with the Bush Administration and the President-elect's team on a threat involving a possible attack on the National Mall during the ceremony.[10] An attack did not materialize, but the identification of a threat emphasized the need for both the outgoing and incoming Administrations to be "well prepared for the events of the day ahead of them" to ensure everyone's safety.[11] The 2009 threat might indicate that, despite the robust nature of the federal government (including, notably, the Department of Defense [DOD] and the Department of Homeland Security [DHS]), America's adversaries may perceive that the United States could be particularly vulnerable during a presidential transition.

Amendments to the PTA have addressed, in part, the need to bolster the federal government's readiness for possible transition-related incidents and the need for the incoming Administration to be prepared to take responsibility for national security immediately following the inauguration. The most recent amendment to the PTA, P.L. 114-136, required the Secretary of Homeland Security to submit a report no later than February 15, 2016, to HSGAC, the House Committee on Organization and Government Reform, and the House Committee on Homeland Security on the "threats and vulnerabilities facing the United States during a presidential transition."[12] Another amendment to the PTA requires the appropriate government officials to provide a summary of "specific operational threats to national security; major military or covert operations; and pending decisions on possible uses of military force" to the President-elect.[13]

Overview of Issues Related to Presidential Transitions

For a sitting President who is not reelected (and barring any electoral disputes), or is concluding a second term, election day marks the beginning of the end of his presidency. While some commentators would argue that a lame duck President can accomplish little during the 11 weeks between election day and inauguration day, William G. Howell and Kenneth R. Mayer offer an alternative perspective:

> Portraits of outgoing presidents going quietly into the night overlook an important feature of American politics, and of executive power—namely, the president's ability to unilaterally set public policy.... Using executive orders, proclamations, executive agreements, national security directives, memoranda, and other directives, presidents

---

[9] Bradley H. Patterson, James P. Pfiffner, and David E. Lewis, *The White House Office of Presidential Personnel*, The White House Transition Project, Report 2009-27, 2008, p. 5, at http://whitehousetransitionproject.org/wp-content/uploads/2016/03/WHTP-2009-27-Presidential-Personnel.pdf.

[10] Ibid., p. 3.

[11] Ibid.

[12] Section 6(a) of P.L. 114-136. The Office of Intelligence and Analysis, Department of Homeland Security, produced the report, *Analysis of Threats and Vulnerabilities During the Presidential Transition*, which is dated August 8, 2016.

[13] Section 7601 of P.L. 108-458 (a)(1).

have at their disposal a wide variety of means to effectuate lasting and substantive policy changes, both foreign and domestic.[14]

Howell and Mayer also note that an outgoing President's level of activity during his final months in office is influenced by the party of his successor. An outgoing President whose successor is from the same political party "has little cause to hurry through a slew of last-minute directives."[15] When the opposing party is poised to regain control of the White House, however, the sitting President might "exercise these powers with exceptional zeal, making final impressions on public policy in the short time" available before inauguration day.[16] Moreover, the incumbent might use the transition period to enact policies and effect changes that might stymie his successor.

> A curious thing happens during the last one hundred days of a presidential administration: political uncertainty shifts to political certitude. The president knows exactly who will succeed him—his policy positions, his legislative priorities, and the level of partisan support he will enjoy within the new Congress. And if the sitting president (or his party) lost the election, he has every reason to hurry through last-minute public policies, doing whatever possible to tie his successor's hands.[17]

During the 20th and 21st centuries, beginning with Theodore Roosevelt, who took office in 1901, there have been 18 presidential transitions, 11 of which were interparty transitions. The Presidents who came into office and replaced a President of another party include the following: Woodrow Wilson, Warren G. Harding, Franklin D. Roosevelt, Dwight D. Eisenhower, John F. Kennedy, Richard M. Nixon, Jimmy Carter, Ronald W. Reagan, William J. Clinton, George W. Bush, and Barack H. Obama.

Regardless of an incumbent President's intentions, however, his decisions and actions in several areas—as well as the activities of his Administration—could affect his successor, and could be a cause for congressional concern. Acting unilaterally, a President can issue executive orders,

---

[14] William G. Howell and Kenneth R. Mayer, "The Last One Hundred Days," *Presidential Studies Quarterly*, vol. 35 (2005), p. 537. Notable examples of "last-minute presidential actions" include the following:

> It was President John Adams's 'Midnight' appointments, which [his successor Thomas] Jefferson refused to honor, that prompted the landmark *Marbury v. Madison* Supreme Court decision. Grover Cleveland created a twenty-one-million-acre forest reserve to prevent logging, an act that lead to an unsuccessful impeachment attempt and the passage of legislation annulling the action. Then, in response to the congressional uprising, 'Cleveland issued a pocket veto and left office'.... Jimmy Carter negotiated for the release of Americans held hostage in Tehran, implementing an agreement on his last day in office with ten separate executive orders, many of which sharply restricted the rights of private parties to sue the Iranian government for expropriation of their property.... In late December 1992, George Bush pardoned six Reagan administration officials who were involved in the Iran-Contra scandal, a step that ended Independent Counsel Lawrence Walsh's criminal investigation. '[In] a single stroke, Mr. Bush swept away one conviction, three guilty pleas, and two pending cases, virtually decapitating what was left of Mr. Walsh's effort, which began in 1986'.... [D]uring his final days in office Clinton 'issued scads of executive orders' on issues ranging from protecting the Hawaiian Islands Coral Reef Ecosystem Reserve to prohibiting the importation of rough cut diamonds from Sierra Leone to curbing tobacco use both domestically and abroad. Ibid., pp. 534-535.

[15] Ibid., p. 538.

[16] Ibid.

[17] Ibid., p. 533. On the other hand, the incumbent Administration might be a significant resource for the President-elect and his team: "One of the most important transition opportunities an incoming President and his team has is the outgoing administration. They are a source of valuable information on personnel positions and can be used to take some actions smoothing the path of the incoming administration." Martha Joynt Kumar et al., *Meeting the Freight Train Head On: Planning for the Transition to Power*, The White House 2001 Project, White House Interview Program, Report No. 2, August 18, 2000, p. 9.

appoint individuals to positions that do not require Senate confirmation (PA positions), and make recess appointments. Additionally, the President can appoint individuals to positions which require Senate approval (PAS positions); the Administration can influence the pace of agency rulemaking; significant decisions regarding presidential and vice presidential records may be made; and some political appointees might be converted to civil service positions in a practice known as "burrowing in."

Depending upon the timing, frequency, content (in the case of executive orders and regulations), and other salient features of certain presidential or Administration actions or decisions, some may question the propriety of an outgoing Administration's actions during the presidential transition period. Certain decisions or actions could affect the incoming President, "forcing [him] to choose between accepting objectionable policies as law or paying a steep political price for trying to change them."[18]

In addition to the possibility of having to address certain actions taken by the outgoing Administration, a new President and his staff have to deal with "the challenges of moving from a campaign to a governing stance," which can include handling "the issues of staffing, management, agenda setting, and policy formulation...."[19] Eager to hit the ground running, an incoming President can use the same tools his predecessor did during the transition period—for example, executive orders, agency rulemaking, and political appointments—to establish his policy agenda, populate the executive branch with his appointees, and possibly overturn or modify some of his predecessor's policies and actions. If the sitting President defers to his successor regarding the submission of a budget, this is an additional task for the newly elected President. Alternatively, if the incumbent submits a budget, his successor may revise it.

In sum, the significance of the transition period for the President-elect cannot be overstated: "Since the advent of the modern presidency under Franklin D. Roosevelt, the actions that presidents-elect undertake before inauguration day have been seen by scholars, journalists, other observers, and even presidents themselves as critical in determining their successes—and failures—once in office."[20]

Congress has a role to play in presidential transitions, though the extent and type of its involvement varies. It is most directly involved in the confirmation of presidential appointees (that is, individuals appointed to PAS positions), the budget process, and, under certain circumstances, oversight of agency rulemaking. Other Administration activities, such as the issuance of executive orders, the disposition of presidential records and vice presidential records, and the granting of pardons, may be of interest to Congress, and, in some cases, might become the subject of congressional oversight or other congressional action. Even the practice of "burrowing in" has warranted congressional interest.

Even though, generally, overlap exists among presidential transition-related topics and issues, the sections in this report are grouped into three categories. Issues that primarily or solely involve the outgoing Administration include personnel (political-to-career conversions), government records, and executive clemency. Cybersecurity and national security are related to the actual transition. The remaining category includes issues that span the outgoing and incoming Administrations:

---

[18] Howell and Mayer, "The Last One Hundred Days," p. 535.

[19] Ibid.

[20] John P. Burke, *Becoming President: The Bush Transition, 2000-2003* (Boulder, CO: Lynne Rienner Publishers, 2004), p. 1.

agency rulemaking, executive branch appointments, judicial branch appointments, executive orders, and submission of the President's budget.

Personnel—Political-to-Career Conversions ("Burrowing In")[21]

Some individuals, who are serving in appointed (noncareer) positions in the executive branch, convert to career positions in the competitive service, the Senior Executive Service (SES), or the excepted service.[22] This practice, commonly referred to as "burrowing in," is permissible when laws and regulations governing career appointments are followed. While such conversions may occur at any time, frequently they do so during the transition period when one Administration is preparing to leave office and another Administration is preparing to assume office.

Generally, these appointees were selected noncompetitively and are serving in such positions as Schedule C,[23] noncareer SES, or limited tenure SES[24] that involve policy determinations or require a close and confidential relationship with the department or agency head and other top officials. Many of the Schedule C appointees receive salaries at the GS-12 through GS-15 pay levels.[25] The noncareer and limited tenure members of the SES receive salaries under the pay schedule for senior executives that also covers the career SES.[26] Career employees, on the other hand, are to be selected on the basis of merit and without political influence following a process that is to be fair and open in evaluating their knowledge, skills, and experience against that of other applicants. The tenure of noncareer and career employees also differs. The former are generally limited to the term of the Administration in which they are appointed or serve at the pleasure of the person who appointed them. The latter constitute a workforce that continues the operations of government without regard to the change of Administrations. In 2007, Paul Light, a professor of government at New York University who studied appointees over several

---

[21] Prepared by (name redacted)   , Analyst in American National Government, Government and Finance Division.

[22] Appointments to career competitive service positions include requirements for approved qualification standards, public announcement of job vacancies, rating of applicants, and completion of a probationary period and three years of continuous service; career SES positions include review by the Office of Personnel Management (OPM) and certification of a candidate's ability by a Qualifications Review Board (QRB); and career excepted service positions allow agencies to establish their own hiring procedures, but require those systems to conform to merit system principles and veterans preference. During agency head transitions, OPM suspends the processing of QRB cases under the authority of 5 C.F.R. §317.502(d). For the policy during the current transition, see U.S. Office of Personnel Management, Memorandum from Beth Cobert, Acting Director, Office of Personnel Management to Agency Heads and Chief Human Capital Officers, "Governmentwide Moratorium on Senior Executive Service (SES) Qualifications Review Board (QRB) Cases," November 18, 2016, available at https://www.chcoc.gov/content/governmentwide-moratorium-senior-executive-service-ses-qualifications-review-board-qrb-cases.

[23] 5 C.F.R. §213.3301.

[24] Appointments to SES positions that have a limited term may be for up to 36 months, and those that are to meet an emergency (unanticipated or urgent need) may be for up to 18 months (5 U.S.C. §3132(a)(5)(6)).

[25] GS refers to the General Schedule, the pay schedule that covers white-collar employees in the federal government. As of January 2017, the salaries from GS-12, step 1, to GS-15, step 10, in the Washington, DC, pay area ranged from $79,720 to $161,900.

[26] Salaries for members of the SES are determined annually by agency heads "under a rigorous performance management system," and range from the minimum rate of basic pay for a senior level (SL) employee (120% of the minimum basic pay rate for GS-15; $124,406, as of January 2017; to either EX Level III ($172,100, as of January 2017); in agencies whose performance appraisal systems have not been certified by OPM as making "meaningful distinctions based on relative performance," or EX Level II ($187,000, as of January 2017); in agencies whose performance appraisal systems have been so certified.

Administrations, indicated that the pay, benefits, and job security of career positions underlie the desire of individuals in noncareer positions to "burrow in."[27]

Beyond the fundamental concern that the conversion of an individual from an appointed (noncareer) position to a career position may not have followed applicable legal and regulatory requirements, "burrowing in" raises other concerns. When the practice occurs, the following perceptions (whether valid or not) may result: that an appointee converting to a career position may limit the opportunity for other employees (who were competitively selected for their career positions, following examination of their knowledge, skills, and experience) to be promoted into another career position with greater responsibility and pay; or that the individual who is converted to a career position may seek to undermine the work of the new Administration whose policies may be at odds with those that he or she espoused when serving in the appointed capacity. Both perceptions may increase the tension between noncareer and career staff and hinder the effective operation of government which relies on career staff to provide the continuity and expertise that underpins it. Public administration literature emphasizes the importance of effective working relationships between noncareer and career staff. In August 2016, for example, the Senior Executives Association (SEA) published a handbook for federal career executives which underscored that members of the SES "are the interface or link between policy and implementation" and stressed that, "An effective working relationship between political appointees and career executives is key to carrying out new initiatives, reforms and improvements of existing programs, and ensuring increased attention to priority services."[28] In addition, SEA's Distinguished Executives Advisory Network developed a series of webinars entitled "Strategies and Best Practices for Managing the Transition to a New Administration, a Webinar Series of Guidance for Career Senior Executives."[29]

Appointments to Career Positions

Appointments to career positions in the executive branch are governed by laws and regulations that are codified in Title 5 of the *United States Code* and Title 5 of the *Code of Federal Regulations*, respectively. For purposes of both, appointments to career positions are among those activities defined as "personnel actions," a class of activities that can be undertaken only in accordance with strict procedures. In taking a personnel action, each department and agency head is responsible for preventing prohibited personnel practices; for complying with, and enforcing, applicable civil service laws, rules, and regulations and other aspects of personnel management; and for ensuring that agency employees are informed of the rights and remedies available to

---

[27] Christopher Lee, "Political Appointees 'Burrowing In,'" *Washington Post*, October 5, 2007, p. A19.

[28] Senior Executives Association, "A Handbook on Presidential Transition for Federal Career Executives," Version 2.0, (Washington, Senior Executives Association, [August 10, 2016], p. 5, at https://seniorexecs.org/images/TransitionHandbook.pdf. Other resources that discuss noncareer and career staff in the federal government include Robert Maranto, *Beyond a Government of Strangers: How Career Executives and Political Appointees Can Turn Conflict to Cooperation* (Lanham: Lexington Books, 2005); Chapters 2, 3, and 7 in Mark A. Abramson and Paul R. Lawrence (eds.), *Learning the Ropes: Insights for Political Appointees* (Lanham: Rowman and Littlefield Publishers, Inc., 2005); G. Edward DeSeve, *Speeding Up the Learning Curve: Observations From a Survey of Seasoned Political Appointees* (Washington: National Academy of Public Administration and the IBM Center for the Business of Government, 2009); Paul R. Lawrence and Mark A. Abramson, *Paths to Making a Difference Leading in Government* (Lanham: Rowman and Littlefield Publishers, Inc., 2011); and Partnership for Public Service, Center for Presidential Transition, "Presidential Transition Guide," January 20, 2016, at http://presidentialtransition.org/publications/viewcontentdetails.php?id=845.

[29] The website for the webinars is https://seniorexecs.org/693-second-webinar-online-what-agencies-are-required-to-do-and-are-doing-now-to-prepare-for-transition.

them. Such actions must adhere to the 9 merit principles and 13 prohibited personnel practices that are codified at 5 U.S.C. §2301(b) and §2302(b), respectively. These principles and practices are designed to ensure that the process for selecting career employees is fair and open (competitive), and free from political influence.

Department and agency heads also must follow regulations, codified at Title 5 of the *Code of Federal Regulations*, that govern career appointments. These include Civil Service Rules 4.2, which prohibits racial, political, or religious discrimination, and 7.1, which addresses an appointing officer's discretion in filling vacancies. Other regulations provide that Office of Personnel Management (OPM) approval is required before employees in Schedule C positions may be detailed to competitive service positions, public announcement is required for all SES vacancies that will be filled by initial career appointment, and details to SES positions that are reserved for career employees (known as Career-Reserved) may only be filled by career SES or career-type non-SES appointees.[30]

During the period June 1, 2016, through January 20, 2017, which is defined as the Presidential Election Period, certain appointees are prohibited from receiving financial awards.[31] These appointees, referred to as senior politically appointed officers, are (1) individuals serving in noncareer SES positions; (2) individuals serving in confidential or policy-determining positions as Schedule C employees; and (3) individuals serving in limited-term and limited emergency positions.

When a department or agency, for example, converts an employee from an appointed (noncareer) position to a career position without any apparent change in duties and responsibilities, or the new position appears to have been tailored to the individual's knowledge and experience, such actions may invite scrutiny. OPM, on an ongoing basis, and GAO, periodically, conduct oversight related to conversions of employees from noncareer to career positions to ensure that proper procedures have been followed.

Office of Personnel Management Approval

A November 5, 2009, memorandum on "Political Appointees and Career Civil Service Positions," issued by then OPM Director John Berry to the heads of departments and agencies, established the policies that govern OPM's oversight of conversions of employees from appointed positions to career positions. The memorandum, citing Section 1104(b)(2) of Title 5, *United States Code*, and Section 5.2 of Title 5, *Code of Federal Regulations*, reiterated that "OPM requires Federal agencies to seek our approval before selecting a political appointee for a competitive service position during a Presidential election year" and "conducts merit staffing reviews of proposed SES appointments whenever they occur."[32] It also noted that, "if the proposed civil service job is below the SES level, OPM's review ha[d] been limited only to competitive service appointments and only those appointments that take place during a Presidential election year."[33]

In a significant change to this policy, the memorandum announced that departments and agencies "must seek prior approval from OPM before they can appoint a current or recent political appointee to a competitive or non-political excepted service position at any level." This policy

---

[30] These regulations are codified at 5 C.F.R. §300.301(c), 5 C.F.R. §317.501, and 5 C.F.R. §317.903(c), respectively.

[31] 5 U.S.C. §4508 and 5 C.F.R. §451.105.

[32] U.S. Office of Personnel Management, Memorandum for Heads of Departments and Agencies, from John Berry, Director, *Political Appointees and Career Civil Service Positions*, November 5, 2009.

[33] Ibid.

became effective on January 1, 2010. A written authorization from OPM is required whenever an department or agency appoints:

> [a] current political Schedule A or Schedule C Executive Branch employee or a former political Schedule A or Schedule C Executive Branch employee who held the position within the last five years to a competitive or non-political excepted service position under title 5 of the U.S. Code; or

> [a] current Non-career SES Executive Branch employee or a former Non-career SES Executive Branch employee who held the position within the last five years to a competitive or non-political excepted service position under title 5 of the U.S. Code.

According to the memorandum, the central personnel agency "will continue to conduct merit staffing reviews for all proposed career SES selections involving a political Schedule A, Schedule C, or non-career SES political appointee before the SES selections are presented to OPM's Qualifications Review Board (QRB) for certification of executive qualifications." OPM reminded agencies "to carefully review all proposed SES selections to ensure they meet merit system principles before such cases are forwarded to the QRB."[34]

OPM Director John Berry explained the policy change by saying that the agency's "responsibility to uphold the merit system is not limited to Presidential election years nor to competitive service appointments."[35] He also said that he "delegated decisionmaking authority over these matters to career Senior Executives at OPM to avoid any hint of political influence."[36] "Pre-Appointment Checklists" for Competitive Service Positions and Non-Political Excepted Service Positions were included as attachments to the OPM memorandum and list the documentation that a department's or agency's Director of Human Resources must submit to OPM along with a dated cover letter.

For the 2016 presidential election year, OPM reminded the heads of departments and agencies of this policy in a memorandum issued on January 11, 2016, by Acting Director Beth Cobert. In Attachment 3 of the memorandum, on the "Do's and Don'ts" of the policy, OPM cautioned departments and agencies not to

> [c]reate or announce a competitive or excepted service vacancy for the sole purpose of selecting a current or former political appointee, Schedule C employee or Noncareer SES employee; or

> [r]emove the Schedule C or Noncareer SES elements of a position solely to appoint the incumbent into the competitive or excepted service.[37]

The January 2016 memorandum also again stated the policies set forth in the November 2009 memorandum.

To assist departments and agencies, OPM also publishes the *Presidential Transition Guide to Federal Human Resources Management Matters*.[38] The most current edition, dated September

---

[34] Ibid.

[35] Ibid.

[36] Ibid.

[37] U.S. Office of Personnel Management, Memorandum for Heads of Departments and Agencies, from Beth Cobert, Acting Director, *Appointments and Awards During the 2016 Presidential Election Period*, January 11, 2016.

[38] U.S. Office of Personnel Management, Presidential Transition Guide to Federal Human Resources Management Matters, September 2016, at https://www.opm.gov/about-us/our-people-organization/support-functions/executive-secretariat/presidential-transition-guide-2016.pdf. OPM posted the document on the agency's website on November 3, 2016.

2016, includes detailed guidance on standards of ethical conduct, appointments, and compensation for federal employees.

New Reporting Requirement for OPM

Section 4(b)(1) of P.L. 114-136 (S. 1172), the Edward "Ted" Kaufman and Michael Leavitt Presidential Transitions Improvement Act of 2015, enacted on March 18, 2016,[39] requires the OPM Director to provide annual reports to the Senate Committee on Homeland Security and Governmental Affairs and the House Committee on Oversight and Government Reform on requests by agencies[40] to appoint political appointees[41] or former political appointees[42] to covered civil service positions.[43] The reports are to cover a calendar year. The law states the data requirements for the reports.

It also requires that certain of the reports be provided quarterly, cover each quarter of the year, and the last quarterly report cover January 1 through January 20 of the following year. Such quarterly reports are required in the last term of a President or in the last year of the second consecutive term of a President, as applicable.

The name or title of a political appointee or a former political appointee may be excluded from a quarterly report if the OPM Director determines that would be appropriate. This circumstance would occur for an appointee who was requested to be appointed to a covered civil service position and was not appointed to a covered civil service position; or to whom a request to be appointed to a covered civil service position is pending at the end of the period covered by the report.

Government Accountability Office Review

Oversight by the GAO focuses on periodic review, after the fact, and, at the request of Congress, of conversions from political to career positions. The agency's most recent evaluation was published on September 30, 2016, and reported on a review of conversions at 30 agencies. The results of that audit covered the period January 1, 2010, through October 1, 2015, and provide the most current retrospective data. Twenty-eight agencies reported 69 conversions. Of that total, 34, or almost 50%, occurred in six agencies—the Departments of Homeland Security (9), Justice (7),

---

[39] Senator Tom Carper introduced S. 1172, the Edward "Ted" Kaufman and Michael Leavitt Presidential Transitions Improvements Act of 2015, on April 30, 2015. The Senate Committee on Homeland Security and Governmental Affairs reported the bill (S.Rept. 114-94) on July 27, 2015. S. 1172 passed the Senate, with amendments, by unanimous consent on July 30, 2015. The House Committee on Oversight and Government Reform reported the bill (H.Rept. 114-384, Part I) on December 18, 2015. The bill had also been referred to the House Committee on Homeland Security which discharged it the same day. The House of Representatives passed S. 1172, amended, under suspension of the rules by voice vote on February 29, 2016. The Senate agreed to the House amendment to the Senate bill by unanimous consent on March 8, 2016.

[40] Agency means an Executive department, a Government corporation, or an independent establishment.

[41] Political appointee means an individual serving in an appointment to a political position. The term political position means an Executive Schedule position, a noncareer appointment in the Senior Executive Service, or a Schedule C position of a confidential or policy-determining character.

[42] Former political appointee means an individual who is not serving in an appointment to a political position, and served as a political appointee during the five-year period ending on the date of the request for an appointment to a covered civil service position in any agency.

[43] Covered civil service position means a position in the civil service that is not a temporary position; or a political position. The civil service consists of all appointive positions in the executive, judicial, and legislative branches, except positions in the uniformed services. 5 U.S.C. §2101.

Defense (5), the Treasury (5), and Health and Human Services (4) and the Federal Deposit Insurance Corporation (4). Twenty-two agencies had three or fewer conversions and two agencies made no conversions. The evaluation found that

> [I]ndividuals were converted from the following categories of noncareer positions: 42 Schedule C positions, 23 noncareer SES positions, 2 presidential appointee positions, 1 limited-term SES position, and 1 administratively determined position.
>
> [R]eported conversions were made to the following categories of career positions: 25 competitive service positions, 29 career SES positions, and 15 career excepted service positions.
>
> Eight agencies converted 17 political appointees (almost 25% of conversions) to career positions without first obtaining OPM approval. Agency officials said they did not seek prior approval from OPM before converting political appointees to career positions because of difficulty understanding OPM's policy for prior approval of political conversions.[44]

Congressional Oversight

As part of its oversight of government operations, Congress also monitors conversions of employees from noncareer to career positions. Such oversight occurred just before and immediately after the presidential election of 2008, and remains ongoing for the presidential election of 2016. During the latter portion of the 114th Congress and the early months of the 115th Congress, oversight included collecting information from federal agencies about hiring during the last two months of the administration of President Barack Obama and appointments that involved conversions from appointed positions to career positions during that administration.

115th Congress

On February 16, 2017, Representative Ken Buck introduced H.R. 1132, the Political Appointee Burrowing Prevention Act, which was referred to the House Committee on Oversight and Government Reform.[45] The bill would establish a two-year prohibition on certain appointees in noncareer positions from accepting positions in the career Civil Service. It seeks to ensure that "federal civil service hiring standards remain solely merit-based, rather than based on political favors."[46]

In January 2017, Representative Jason Chaffetz, Chairman of the House Committee on Oversight and Government Reform, sent letters to each of the Cabinet departments and the Environmental Protection Agency, the General Services Administration, the Office of Management and Budget, and the Small Business Administration. Each of the letters requested the same information: "(1) A

---

[44] U.S. Government Accountability Office, *Office of Personnel Management: Actions Are Needed to Help Ensure the Completeness of Political Conversion Data and Adherence to Policy*, GAO-16-859 (Washington: GAO, September 30, 2016), pp. 8 and 9, at http://www.gao.gov/assets/690/680178.pdf. The Department of Homeland Security had the highest number (6) of conversions made without OPM approval. For earlier GAO evaluations, see U.S. Government Accountability Office, *Personnel Practices: Conversions of Employees from Political to Career Positions May 2005-May 2009*, GAO-10-688, (Washington: GAO, June 2010) and U.S. Government Accountability Office, *Conversions of Selected Employees from Political to Career Positions at Departments and Selected Agencies*, GAO-10-356R, (Washington: GAO, January 29, 2010).

[45] Representatives Ted Lieu and Jared Polis cosponsored the bill.

[46] Representative Ken Buck, Press Release, "Buck and Lieu Introduce Bill to Prevent Burrowing into Federal Civil Service Positions," February 16, 2017, at https://buck.house.gov/media-center/press-releases/buck-and-lieu-introduce-bill-prevent-burrowing-federal-civil-service.

list of all job openings, GS-13 and higher, announced since November 9, 2016;[47] (2) All documents submitted to OPM referring or relating to employee hiring after November 9, 2016, including any and all documents seeking Direct-Hire Authority or approval to convert non-career political staff to career positions; and (3) For each GS-13 position opening during calendar year 2015, the number of days between the vacancy announcement and the date the Department selected a candidate."[48] Representative Chaffetz, citing a news report in the *Washington Post* that stated "Federal agencies are accelerating the hiring of civil service positions and compressing hiring timelines in anticipation of a possible hiring freeze in 2017," said that "Hiring decisions must be legitimate, justified, and free from political influence."[49]

114th Congress

On December 2, 2016, Senator Ron Johnson, Chairman of the Senate Committee on Homeland Security and Governmental Affairs, and Senator Thom Tillis sent a letter to President Obama encouraging him to consider "the implementation of a hiring freeze on all career civil servant positions, except those that involve public health or safety, until the end of [his] term." The letter stated that, "Not only is 'burrowing in' unfair to applicants without an inside connection, it further contributes to the possibility that federal workers may attempt to undermine the policies of the new president." The Senators expressed the hope that, by taking such an action, the President would "set a precedent for future presidential transitions."[50]

Earlier, on November 21, 2016, Senator Johnson sent a letter to Acting OPM Director Beth Cobert requesting "(1) A list of all federal employees who have converted from political appointments to career positions during the period of June 30, 2016, and the date of your response,"[51] and "(2) A weekly update of all conversions and requests for conversions from political appointments to career positions that occur between the date of your response, and January 20, 2017."[52] The letter expressed the Senator's view that "we must guard against inappropriate hiring practices to ensure merit-based federal employment and protect the independence of the federal civil service."[53]

---

[47] The letter specified the information to be provided for each position: the job announcement, including name and grade of the position; the description of the position, including any necessary skills and qualifications; the number of applicants; whether the position was a competitive service position, and if so, the number of individuals that were on the certification list for each such position; and the date of hire.

[48] The letters requested that the information be provided by January 19, 2017. For example, Letter from Representative Jason Chaffetz to Sally Jewell, Secretary, Department of the Interior, January 10, 2017, at https://oversight.house.gov/wp-content/uploads/2017/01/2017-01-10-JEC-to-18-Agencies-Agency-Hiring-due-1-19-18-letters.pdf.

[49] Ibid.

[50] Letter from Senators Ron Johnson and Thom Tillis to President Barack Obama, December 2, 2016, at https://www.tillis.senate.gov/public/index.cfm/press-releases?ID=EF043932-8E4A-4474-BF8B-F1284FED6C41.

[51] The letter specified the contents for the list as follows: employee's full name and first date of employment at the department or agency; all job titles held by the employee throughout his or her tenure at the department or agency, and the dates of any title changes; all salaries received by the employee throughout his or her tenure at the department or agency and the dates of any salary changes; date on which the employee transitioned to a career position within the department or agency. In addition, for any conversions for which OPM conducts a post-appointment review, the letter requested that OPM provide: OPM's findings from the review; recommendations provided by OPM to the violating agency; corrective actions taken by the violating agency; and whether the political appointee remained in the same career position. Senator Johnson requested a response by December 1, 2016.

[52] The letter specified that the weekly update should include the same information as the initial list.

[53] Letter from Senator Ron Johnson to Acting OPM Director Beth Cobert, November 21, 2016, at https://www.hsgac.senate.gov/media/majority-media/johnson-requests-that-opm-be-wary-of-political-appointees-burrowing-in-to-career-positions-during-transition.

Also on February 16, 2016, Senator Orrin Hatch, Chairman of the Senate Finance Committee, and Representative Kevin Brady, Chairman of the House Ways and Means Committee, sent letters to the Department of Health and Human Services, the Department of the Treasury, the U.S. Trade Representative, and the Social Security Administration requesting information on personnel conversions of noncareer employees. Specifically, the letters requested information on "every non-career employee[54] who has converted from [a] non-career position to a career or non-political excepted service position" within the respective department or agency, from the respective department or agency to another government agency, or from another agency to the respective department or agency, from January 1, 2009, to the present.[55] The letters also requested that the departments and agencies "provide the Committees with a list of all corrective actions[56] requested by OPM as a result of the pre-employment review process and the status of those actions."[57]

Four Members of Congress requested the GAO review discussed above under the section on Government Accountability Office Review. In a November 30, 2015, letter to Eugene Dodaro, Comptroller General, Senator Johnson; Senator John Thune, chairman of the Senate Committee on Commerce, Science, and Transportation; Representative Fred Upton, chairman of the House Committee on Energy and Commerce; and Representative Chaffetz, had asked GAO to review political appointee conversions to career federal civil service positions from June 1, 2009, through October 1, 2015. The Members also asked GAO to review the implementation and effectiveness of the OPM policy that became effective on January 1, 2010. The letter included additional requirements for GAO's review and suggested that "the GAO continue to conduct periodic reviews in the future to ensure consistent application of these rules."[58] It noted that the Members requested the study because "The possibility that political appointees are 'burrowing in'—through favoritism in the selection process, effectively taking civil positions that would otherwise be open to the public and awarded based on merit—may affect the integrity of the merit-based federal workforce."[59]

The next day, Timothy Dirks, then interim president of the Senior Executives Association, sent a letter to the Senators commending them for requesting the GAO review. According to Mr. Dirks:

> SEA is particularly concerned about burrowing in to SES and equivalent positions. As you know, the positions that Senior Executives hold are some of the most difficult and complex in the federal government and require expertise that is built up from years of experience. We have seen some cases where political employees or candidates for employment are placed in Senior Executive positions for which they may be unqualified or less qualified than other candidates, or where their service as political appointees was given undue weight. Most of those experienced with the federal personnel system

---

[54] A noncareer employee includes, but is not limited to, a political appointee, Senior Executive Service employee, senior-level employee, and scientific or professional employee.

[55] The letters requesting the information are at U.S. Congress, Senate Committee on Finance, "Hatch, Brady Call on Federal Agencies to Prevent Political Employee 'Burrowing,'" February 17, 2016, at http://www.finance.senate.gov/chairmans-news/hatch-brady-call-on-federal-agencies-to-prevent-political-employee-burrowing. (Hereinafter referred to as Hatch, Brady Letters.)

[56] 5 U.S.C. §1103(a)(5) provides that the Director of the Office of Personnel Management is to execute, administer, and enforce the civil service rules and regulations and the laws governing the civil service.

[57] Hatch, Brady Letters.

[58] The letter requesting the review is available at U.S. Congress, Senate Committee on Homeland Security and Governmental Affairs, "Senate and House Leaders Seek GAO Review of Political Appointee Conversions to Federal Civil Service Positions," November 30, 2015, at https://www.hsgac.senate.gov/media/majority-media/senate-and-house-leaders-seek-gao-review-of-political-appointee-conversions-to-federal-civil-service-positions.

[59] Ibid.

understand that this can be attempted through hiring actions with limited competitive areas of consideration, short announcement times and narrowly defined statements of required technical qualifications. Political influence and pressure can also contribute non-meritorious selections. We fully understand that some political appointees who make the switch to the career civil service may be the best candidates for the position, and believe that providing transparency and sunlight to the conversion process can aid in preventing its abuse.[60]

Upon publication of GAO's September 30, 2016, findings, Representatives Upton and Chaffetz and Senators Thune and Johnson issued a joint press release on October 6, 2016, which stated, in part,

"Rules exist for a reason. The nonpartisan watchdog's findings that one out of every four political appointees who burrowed into the executive branch during this administration did not follow the rules is deeply troubling," said Upton. "GAO's guidance should help ensure proper procedures are followed so favoritism and bias are free from the inner workings of our government."

"Hiring decisions must be free from political interference, legitimate, and justified," said Chaffetz. "OPM should fully embrace GAO's recommendation for a more stringent process to verify all conversions are appropriate. Fair and open competition is central to the integrity of a merit-based federal workforce."

"One of the reasons the federal government has laws on merit-based hiring is to prevent cronyism and political favoritism," said Thune. "GAO's finding that the Obama administration hasn't consistently followed these rules is troubling."

"The practice of burrowing in threatens the integrity of the federal workforce, where employees need to be hired based on merit and not on partisan political beliefs," said Johnson. "I was particularly disappointed to see the Department of Homeland Security reporting the highest number of appointee-to-career employee conversions. It is critical that the administration take steps to ensure fairness and competition in federal service."[61]

Issues for Congressional Consideration

In assessing the current situation, Congress may decide that the existing oversight is sufficient. If Congress determines that additional measures are needed to ensure that conversions from appointed (noncareer) positions to career positions are conducted according to proper procedures and are transparent, OPM could be directed to report to Congress on the operation of its current policy governing pre-appointment reviews, including recommendations on whether Section 1104 of Title 5, *United States Code*[62] should be amended to codify the policy. Congress also could direct the central personnel agency to report on whether any changes are needed, in the Presidential Election Period, that restrict financial awards to senior politically appointed officers.

---

[60] Letter from Timothy M. Dirks to Senator Ron Johnson, Chairman of the Senate Committee on Homeland Security and Governmental Affairs; Senator John Thune, Chairman of the Senate Committee on Commerce, Science, and Transportation; Representative Fred Upton, Chairman of the House Committee on Energy and Commerce; and Representative Jason Chaffetz, Chairman of the House Committee on Oversight and Government Reform, December 1, 2015, at https://seniorexecs.org/images/documents/policy_letters/SEALettertoChairmenonBurrowingIn00060860x87C30.pdf.

[61] U.S. Congress, House Committee on Energy and Commerce, Press Release, "House and Senate Requestors Issue Statement on GAO Political 'Burrowing' Review Findings," October 3, 2016, at https://energycommerce.house.gov/news-center/press-releases/house-and-senate-requestors-issue-statement-gao-political-burrowing.

[62] 5 U.S.C. §1104, in part, covers delegations of authority for personnel management from the President to the Director of the Office of Personnel Management and from the director to agency heads.

From Election to Inauguration—An Overview of the Process 49

As discussed above, the dates of the Presidential Election Period are defined by law, and, in a presidential election year, cover the period from June 1 through the following January 20. Congress also could increase the penalties for violating civil service laws by "creat[ing] a misdemeanor offense for agency personnel who violate or contribute to the violation of the federal hiring statutes"[63] or examine whether Title 5 of the *United States Code* should be amended to prohibit conversion from political to career positions. Given the findings of GAO's most recent evaluation that almost 25% of conversions to career positions occurred without agencies first obtaining OPM approval and that the agencies said that they did not seek such prior approval because of difficulty understanding OPM's policy,[64] Congress could direct OPM or the Chief Human Capital Officers Council to provide training to federal managers and supervisors on the policy. With the continuing interest of Congress, and particularly the House Committee on Oversight and Government Reform and the Senate Committee on Homeland Security and Governmental Affairs, in exercising oversight of conversions from appointed positions to career positions, Congress could consider directing OPM to provide standardized reports on a regular bases to Congress, or maintain such information where it could be easily and securely accessed by Congress.

Government Records[65]

When a President leaves office, he and his Administration have likely generated millions of government records—some of which may be of long-term interest to Congress, federal agencies, incoming Presidents, researchers, and members of the general public. This section provides information on the laws and policies that govern these records. The section is divided into two topics—agency federal records and presidential records—because both types of records are generated during a presidential Administration and federal law places unique requirements on each.

Federal Records

Pursuant to the Federal Records Act (FRA; Chapters 21, 29, 31, and 33 of Title 44 of the U.S. Code), federal agency records in all three branches are to be created, retained, preserved, and accessed differently than records that qualify as presidential records, records of Congress, or Supreme Court records.[66] Responsibility for guiding and assisting the life-cycle management of federal government records rests with the Archivist of the United States, who is the head of the National Archives and Records Administration (NARA).

The transition from one presidential Administration to another may prompt concerns that some federal records could be lost, improperly destroyed, or removed.[67] These concerns are heightened

---

[63] Lauren Mendolera, "How to Stop a Mole: A Look at Burrowing in the Federal Civil Service," *New York University Journal of Legislation and Public Policy*, Vol. 13:643, 2010, see pp. 665-671.

[64] U.S. Government Accountability Office, *Office of Personnel Management: Actions Are Needed to Help Ensure the Completeness of Political Conversion Data and Adherence to Policy*, GAO-16-859 (Washington: GAO, September 30, 2016), p. 9, at http://www.gao.gov/assets/690/680178.pdf.

[65] Prepared by (name redacted), Analyst in American National Government, Government and Fi nance Division.

[66] Laws and policies that govern presidential records are discussed in the section below.

[67] A 1989 General Accounting Office (GAO) report found that some senior Cabinet officials sought to remove federal records upon leaving office. See U.S. General Accounting Office, *Federal Records: Removal of Agency Documents by Senior Officials Upon Leaving Office*, GAO/GGD-89-91, July 1989, at http://gao.gov/assets/150/148058.pdf. Proper management of federal records, regardless of the election cycle remains a concern for both NARA and the Government (continued...)

by the increasing number of platforms on which records can be created (e.g., Facebook, Instagram, iTunes, Flickr, Google+, Twitter, YouTube) and the increasing storage volume of records.[68] Since the most recent presidential transition in January 2009, several changes have occurred that directly affect the collection and retention of federal agency records. Among these changes were the enactment of a new definition of federal records and the Administration's release of various policy documents instructing executive branch agencies on various recordkeeping requirements.

A New Definition for Federal Records

Of particular concern for the 2016 transition is the updated definition of federal records, as amended by the Presidential and Federal Records Act Amendments of 2014 (P.L. 113-187).[69] The new definition of federal *records* reads as follows:

> Records includes all recorded information,[70] regardless of form or characteristics, made or received by a Federal agency under Federal law or in connection with the transaction of public business and preserved or appropriate for preservation by that agency or its legitimate successor as evidence of the organization, functions, policies, decisions, procedures, operations, or other activities of the Government or because of the informational value of the data in them.

According to the congressional reports to accompany P.L. 113-187, the amended definition of federal records seeks to "shift the emphasis away from the physical media used to store information to the actual information being stored, regardless of form or characteristic."[71]

(...continued)

Accountability Office. In 2008, for example, GAO determined that "e-mail records were not being appropriately identified and preserved" at certain federal agencies. U.S. Government Accountability Office, *Federal Records: Agencies Face Challenges in Managing E-Mail*, GAO-08-699T, April 23, 2008, preliminary findings, at http://www.gao.gov/assets/120/119711.pdf. In April 2010, NARA published a report on agencies' self-assessments of their recordkeeping Administration. The report found that 95% of agencies were rated as having moderate to high risk of improper records management. National Archives and Records Administration, *2010 Records Management Self-Assessment Report*, Washington, DC, February 22, 2011, p. 5, at http://www.archives.gov/records-mgmt/pdf/rm-self-assessmemt.pdf. The study included 251 respondent agencies and found a 25% to 27% error rate in certain survey responses, which NARA stated "raises questions more about the accuracy of the scores for individual agencies than for the results of the overall survey." Ibid., p. 2. In June 2010, GAO testified that federal records management "has received low priority within the federal government." U.S. Government Accountability Office, *Information Management: The Challenges of Maintaining Electronic Records*, GAO-10-838T, June 17, 2010, p. 17, at http://www.gao.gov/assets/130/124883.pdf. In June 2011, GAO found that many agencies lacked a formal policy on how to capture and maintain federal records created on social media. U.S. Government Accountability Office, *Social Media: Federal Agencies Need Policies and Procedures for Managing and Protecting Information They Access and Disseminate*, GAO-11-605, June 2011, at http://gao.gov/assets/330/320244.pdf.

[68] In its *Electronic Records Project, Summary Report for FY2005-FY2009*, NARA wrote that "[w]ith the volume and complexity of e-records increasing each year, it continues to be a challenge for both NARA and [f]ederal agencies to keep pace with the requirements to identify, schedule, and transfer to NARA all existing records." National Archives and Records Administration, *NARA's Electronic Records Project, Summary Report FY2005-FY2009*, p. 13, Washington, DC, June 15, 2010, at http://www.archives.gov/records-mgmt/resources/e-records-report.pdf.

[69] For more details on the Presidential and Federal Records Act Amendments of 2014, see CRS Report R43072, *Common Questions About Federal Records and Related Agency Requirements*, by (name redacted) .

[70] *Recorded information* is further defined in 44 U.S.C. §3301 as "all traditional forms of records, regardless of physical form or characteristics, including information created, manipulated, communicated, or stored in digital or electronic form."

[71] U.S. Congress, Senate Committee on Homeland Security and Governmental Affairs, *Presidential and Federal Records Act Amendments of 2014*, 113th Cong., 2nd sess., July 23, 2014, S.Rept. 113-218 (Washington: GPO, 2014), p. 5.

Previously, the statutory definition of records included references to certain types of materials or platforms on which records could be created or captured, such as "books, papers, photographs" and "machine-readable formats." The amended definition, instead, refers more generically to "recorded information."

Federal agency staff will have to ensure that records that meet this new definition are appropriately captured and retained for as long as necessary, pursuant to law, regulation, and internal agency policies. The transition to a new President may not appear to directly affect the collection and retention of federal records at executive branch agencies because laws governing federal records, as defined above, are not contingent upon the start and end of presidential tenures. At the end of any presidential Administration, however, many political appointees in federal agencies will leave their positions. Upon their departure from federal service, these appointees will have to ensure that the federal records they have created are properly managed and preserved pursuant to the Federal Records Act.[72]

Those appointed to political positions at federal agencies within the new Administration will also have to apply the provisions of the Federal Records Act to information they generate as part of their job responsibilities. Additionally, the Obama Administration is the first to have used such a varied array of electronic platforms, making collection, retention, and future access to records created by and during the Obama Administration more complex. This complexity manifests in the release of various records collection and retention guidance issued during the Obama Administration, which will be described in greater detail below.

Administration Recordkeeping Guidance and Requirements

In addition to implementing the new statutory definition of a federal record, federal government agencies will also be responsible for applying NARA's records management guidance, directives, and bulletins to existing and new federal records. Many of the NARA policy documents have addressed concerns related to the rapid growth of records in an increasing variety of electronic formats.

Among the more prominent policies published during the Obama Administration was the 2012 "Managing Government Records Directive." This directive, issued jointly by NARA and OMB, required, among other things, that all executive branch agencies must manage all email records in an electronic format by the end of 2016, and manage all permanent electronic records electronically by 2019.[73] The directive also called on federal officials to work with private industry to "produce economically viable automated records management" options, including technologies that would be "suitable approaches for the automated management of email, social media, and other types of digital record content."[74] In May 2015, GAO released a report stating that of the 24 agencies examined, 5 had yet to meet the directive's requirements.[75]

---

[72] FRA; 44 U.S.C. Chapters 21, 29, 31, and 33.

[73] In 2014, a majority of federal agencies (73%, 188 agencies) reported using a "print and file" method of manage email records. See U.S. National Archives and Records Administration, "Records Management Self-Assessment 2014," p. Appendix II-29, at http://www.archives.gov/records-mgmt/resources/self-assessment-2014.pdf.

[74] See Jeffrey D. Zients and David S. Ferriero, *Managing Government Records Directive*, U.S. Office of Management and Budget and National Archives and Records Administration, M-12-18, Washington, DC, August 24, 2012, at http://www.whitehouse.gov/sites/default/files/omb/memoranda/2012/m-12-18.pdf.

[75] U.S. Government Accountability Office, *Information Management: Additional Actions Are Needed to Meet Requirements of the Managing Government Records Directive*, GAO-15-339, May 2015, at http://gao.gov/assets/680/670195.pdf.

In 2013, NARA established the Capstone approach to help agencies meet the 2016 deadline for managing email electronically.[76] The Capstone approach suggests that agencies may manage email collection and retention based on the email account holder, rather than by the individual content of the email records. The approach calls for the automated capture of the email accounts of senior agency officials, thereby treating their emails presumptively as permanent records. Under this approach, other agency employee email accounts would be maintained as generating temporary records for a set period of time, for example, seven years. In 2013 and 2014, NARA also released guidance concerning the unlawful removal of records,[77] managing social media records,[78] and managing email records.[79]

NARA's Administration Transition Bulletins

In previous presidential election years, NARA issued a bulletin reminding agency heads of the regulations regarding proper records management.[80] Previous NARA bulletins have focused on which records are to remain in the custody of executive departments and agencies, and which ones may be removed by the outgoing Administration.

The 2008 bulletin, for example, stated that departing officials and employees could remove extra copies of records when they left their agencies "with the approval of a designated official of the agency, such as the agency's records officer or legal counsel."[81] The bulletin, however, reminded readers that if such materials were otherwise restricted—for example, because they contained personally identifiable information or classified material—they "must be maintained in accordance with the appropriate agency requirements."[82] The bulletin provided additional guidance detailing how to identify a federal record, how to properly store or dispose of qualifying records, and how to respond to the unauthorized removal of records. Criminal penalties can be

---

[76] National Archives and Records Administration, *Guidance on a New Approach to Managing Email Records*, NARA Bulletin 2013-02, April 29, 2013, at http://www.archives.gov/records-mgmt/bulletins/2013/2013-02.html.

[77] National Archives and Records Administration, Guidance for Agency Employees on the Management of Federal Records, Including Email Accounts, and the Protection of Federal Records from Unauthorized Removal, NARA Bulletin 2013-03, September 9, 2013, at http://www.archives.gov/records-mgmt/bulletins/2013/2013-03.html. This guidance superseded Allen Weinstein, Protecting Federal Records and Other Documentary Materials from Unauthorized Removal, National Archives and Records Administration, NARA Bulletin 2008-02, Washington, DC, February 4, 2008, at http://www.archives.gov/records-mgmt/bulletins/2008/2008-02.html.

[78] National Archives and Records Administration, *Guidance on Managing Social Media Records*, NARA Bulletin 2014-02, October 25, 2013, at http://www.archives.gov/records-mgmt/bulletins/2014/2014-02.html.

[79] David Ferriero, National Archives and Records Administration, *Guidance on Managing Email*, NARA Bulletin 2014-06, September 15, 2014, at http://www.archives.gov/records-mgmt/bulletins/2014/2014-06.html; National Archives and Records Administration, *Guidance on Managing Email*.

[80] As stated in the first line of the 2008 bulletin, which was issued on February 4, 2008, its purpose "is to remind heads of Federal agencies that official records must remain in the custody of the agency." National Archives and Records Administration, *Protecting Federal Records and Other Documentary Materials from Unauthorized Removal*, NARA Bulletin 2008-02, February 4, 2008, at http://www.archives.gov/records-mgmt/bulletins/2008/2008-02.html?template=print. NARA did not release such a bulletin in 2012, a presidential election year in which President Obama was reelected.

[81] National Archives and Records Administration, *Protecting Federal Records and Other Documentary Materials from Unauthorized Removal*, NARA Bulletin 2008-02, February 4, 2008, at http://www.archives.gov/records-mgmt/bulletins/2008/2008-02.html?template=print.

[82] Ibid.

From Election to Inauguration—An Overview of the Process

levied for the unauthorized removal or destruction of, concealment of,[83] and unauthorized disclosure of federal records.[84]

In February 2016, NARA re-issued its long-standing guidance on "Documenting Your Public Service" to assist federal employees in the proper management of federal records. This guidance also stated that "It is important for agencies to ensure employees are aware of their records management responsibilities, especially as we approach the upcoming Presidential transition."[85]

Presidential Records

For almost two centuries, the official papers of Presidents were considered their personal property, which they could take with them when they departed from office. That practice changed with the Presidential Records Act of 1978 (PRA), which establishes that all presidential records created on or after January 20, 1981, were automatically government property that would transfer into the legal and physical control of the Archivist when a President leaves office.[86] The statute also covers the official records of the Vice President.[87] Pursuant to the PRA, incumbent Presidents are responsible for managing their records during the tenure of their Administrations. The act applies to the records of Presidents dating back to President Reagan.[88] A 2008 article written by NARA's Director of the Presidential Materials Staff stated that

> NARA works with White House and vice presidential counsels, the White House Office of Records Management, the National Security Council, the White House Gifts Office, and other White House offices and the Office of the Vice President to receive approval to move early and to coordinate on what records and artifacts can move when. Additionally, throughout the presidential administration, these offices have worked to establish initial control and arrangement over the records and artifacts, provide preliminary descriptions at the folder, box, or artifact level, and to ready these materials for eventual transfer to NARA.[89]

The PRA defines *presidential records* as "documentary materials ... created or received by the President, the President's immediate staff, or a unit or individual of the Executive Office of the President whose function is to advise or assist the President."[90] In turn, the term *documentary materials* includes

> all books, correspondence, memorandums, documents, papers, pamphlets, works of art, models, pictures, photographs, plats, maps, films, and motion pictures, including, but not

---

[83] 18 U.S.C. §2071.

[84] 5 U.S.C. §552a(i); 18 U.S.C. §793-794, 798.

[85] National Archives and Records Administration, "Documenting Your Public Service," at http://www.archives.gov/records-mgmt/publications/documenting-your-public-service.html.

[86] 44 U.S.C. §§2201-2207. The records for President Ronald Reagan were the first records governed by the Presidential Records Act.

[87] 44 U.S.C. §2207.

[88] All presidential records in federal presidential libraries dedicated to the records of Presidents who served prior to Ronald Reagan (Herbert Hoover through Jimmy Carter) are materials donated to the libraries' collections. Those records are released according to the dictates of the applicable President (if he is living) or the dictates of the families of the former President (if he is deceased). For more information on presidential libraries, see CRS Report R41513, *The Presidential Libraries Act and the Establishment of Presidential Libraries*, by (name redacted), (name redacted), and (name redacted) .

[89] Nancy Kegan Smith, "Escorting a Presidency into History: NARA's Role in a White House Transition," *Prologue Magazine*, Winter 2008, vol. 40, no. 4, at http://www.archives.gov/publications/prologue/2008/winter/transitions.html.

[90] 44 U.S.C. §2201(2).

limited to, audio, audiovisual, or other electronic or mechanical recordations, whether in analog, digital, or any other form.[91]

The statute further states, "Nothing in this Act shall be construed to confirm, limit, or expand any constitutionally-based privilege which may be available to an incumbent or former President."[92] This provision constituted a recognition of the President's historical, constitutionally based privilege to exercise discretion regarding the provision of information sought by another co-equal branch of the federal government—that is, executive privilege.[93]

For FY2017, the Executive Office of the President's Office of Administration requested $7.6 million "for data migration services for processing of records of the department President and Vice President ... and for other transition-related administrative expenses."[94]

Amendments to the Presidential Records Act

Successive presidential Administrations have interpreted the PRA differently.[95] In November 2014, Congress enacted and President Obama signed into law the Presidential and Federal Records Act Amendments of 2014 (P.L. 113-187), which codifies some parts of the PRA that have historically been interpreted in various ways by incumbent Presidents.

The law, among other things, amended the PRA to explicitly provide a 60-day review period to the incumbent and applicable former President any time the Archivist intends to publicly release previously unreleased presidential records. The review period can be extended for an additional 30 days if the Archivist receives a statement from the incumbent or former President that "such an extension is necessary to allow an adequate review of the record."[96] The law also codified the requirement that any claim of executive privilege must be made by the applicable former President or by the incumbent President.[97] P.L. 113-187 also prohibits anyone convicted of inappropriately using, removing, or destroying NARA records from accessing presidential records.

Growth in Records and Volume

Pursuant to the PRA, presidential records are provided to NARA at the end of each presidential Administration.[98] As a result, NARA has tracked the increasing volume and varied electronic formats employed by each Administration.

In June 2010, GAO submitted testimony to the House Committee on Oversight and Government Reform's Subcommittee on Information Policy, Census, and National Archives on "The

---

[91] 44 U.S.C. §2201(1).

[92] 44 U.S.C. §2204(c)(2).

[93] See (name redacted)*The Politics of Executive Privilege* (Durham, NC: Carolina Academic Press, 2004); and Mark J. Rozell, *Executive Privilege: Presidential Power, Secrecy, and Accountability*, 2nd ed., rev. (Lawrence, KS: University Press of Kansas, 2002).

[94] Executive Office of the President, *Congressional Budget Submission: Fiscal Year 2017*, Washington, DC, 2016, p. AS-3, at https://www.whitehouse.gov/sites/default/files/docs/fy2017eopbudgetfinalelectronic.pdf.

[95] See E.O. 12667; E.O. 13233; and E.O. 13489.

[96] 44 U.S.C. §2208(a)(3)(B).

[97] H.R. 1144 and H.R. 3071, both introduced in the 112th Congress, included similar provisions.

[98] 44 U.S.C. §§2201-2207. NARA is to be provided the universe of qualifying presidential records at the end of each Administration.

Challenges of Managing Electronic Records." GAO stated that the "[h]uge volumes of electronic information" were a "major challenge" in agency record management.[99]

> Electronic information is increasingly being created in volumes that pose a significant technical challenge to our ability to organize it and make it accessible. An example of this growth is provided by the difference between the digital records of the George W. Bush administration and that of the Clinton administration: NARA has reported that the Bush administration transferred 77 terabytes[100] of data to the [National] Archives [and Records Administration] on leaving office, which was about 35 times the amount of data transferred by the Clinton administration.[101]

On April 25, 2013, a NARA blog post provided additional details on the records being transferred to the George W. Bush Library and Museum in Dallas, TX—"more than 70 million pages of textual records, 43,000 artifacts, 200 million emails (totaling roughly 1 billion pages), and 4 million digital photographs (the largest holding of electronic records of any of our libraries)."[102]

Pursuant to the PRA, NARA is responsible for the custody, control, and preservation of the records of former Presidents. NARA has worked with incumbent Presidents as they prepare to leave office to ensure the capture and preservation of records generated through social media. Examples may be found in the preserved *whitehouse.gov* content available through the websites of the Clinton and George W. Bush Libraries.[103]

In 2015, Archivist David Ferriero stated in a NARA blog about the forthcoming Barack Obama Presidential Library that

> [t]he transfer of electronic records is one of the most complex and challenging parts of a presidential transition since the volume and variety of records generated or received by presidential administrations has increased exponentially.[104]

---

[99] U.S. Government Accountability Office, *Information Management: The Challenges of Managing Electronic Records*, GAO-10-838T, June 17, 2010, p. 10, at http://gao.gov/assets/130/124883.pdf.

[100] A terabyte is about 1 trillion bytes, or 1,000 gigabytes.

[101] U.S. Government Accountability Office, *Information Management: The Challenges of Managing Electronic Records*, p. 10. GAO stated in its written testimony that it did not independently verify these reported volumes of records.

[102] National Archives and Records Administration, "Prologue: Pieces of History," April 25, 2013, at http://blogs.archives.gov/prologue/?p=12073. The George H.W. Bush Presidential Library and Museum, by comparison, contains 1 million photographs and 10,000 videotapes. See George H.W. Bush Presidential Library and Museum, "FAQs," at http://bushlibrary.tamu.edu/research/faq.php.

[103] Information provided electronically to the author by NARA on March 21, 2014. The George W. Bush websites archive is at http://georgewbush-whitehouse.archives.gov, and the William J. Clinton websites archive is at http://clintonlibrary.gov/_previous/archivesearch.html.

[104] David Ferriero, "Creating the Obama Library," *Prologue Magazine*, vol. 47, no. 3 (Fall 2015), at https://www.archives.gov/publications/prologue/2015/fall/archivist.html. For more on the establishment of a presidential library for President Obama, see CRS Report R41513, *The Presidential Libraries Act and the Establishment of Presidential Libraries*, by (name redacted), (name redacted), and (name redacted) .

Executive Clemency[105]

Background

Article II of the Constitution provides the President with the explicit authority to "grant Reprieves and Pardons for Offences against the United States." The general term for this authority is executive clemency, of which the more commonly used term, presidential pardon, is but one form. Executive clemency may also take the form of commutation, which is the reduction of a prison sentence; remission, which is the reduction of a fine or mandated restitution; or reprieve, which delays the imposition of punishment.[106]

The President has few restrictions on how and when executive clemency may be exercised, other than it may only apply to violations of federal laws—thereby precluding state criminal or civil proceedings from its scope—and it may not be used to interfere with Congress's power to impeach.[107] Clemency in the form of a pardon, for example, may be granted at any time, even before charges have been filed.[108] In addition, while not frequently done, a President may bestow clemency on groups, as President Abraham Lincoln did when he issued a pardon to all persons who participated in the "rebellion" against the United States (with a number of conditions and exceptions).[109]

The President's use of this broad authority may come under increased scrutiny during a period of transition, in part because Presidents have historically granted petitions for clemency at a higher rate in the closing months of their Administrations. **Table 1** shows that since 1945, every President that completed his term of office, except President Lyndon B. Johnson, increased the rate at which he granted clemency in the final four months of his Administration, when compared to his previous months in office.

Table 1. Average Monthly Clemency Petitions Granted, Prior to and During the Final Four Months of Selected Administrations

President	Prior to Final Four Months of Administration	Final Four Months of Administration
Harry S. Truman	22 per month	25 per month
Dwight D. Eisenhower	10 per month	53 per month
Lyndon B. Johnson	21 per month	0 per month
Gerald R. Ford	11 per month	34 per month
Jimmy Carter	11 per month	20 per month
Ronald W. Reagan	4 per month	8 per month
George H.W. Bush	1 per month	10 per month
William J. Clinton	2 per month	65 per month

---

[105] Prepared by (name redacted), Specialist in American National Government, Government and Finance Division.

[106] U.S. Department of Justice, Office of the Pardon Attorney, at http://www.usdoj.gov/pardon/.

[107] CRS Report RS20829, *An Overview of the Presidential Pardoning Power*, by (name redacted), available upon request.

[108] Ibid.

[109] U.S. President (Lincoln), "The Proclamation of Amnesty and Reconstruction," December 8, 1863, at http://www.history.umd.edu/Freedmen/procamn.htm.

President	Prior to Final Four Months of Administration	Final Four Months of Administration
George W. Bush	2 per month	8 per month
Barack Obama	8 per month	300 per month

Source: U.S. Department of Justice, Office of the Pardon Attorney, at http://www.usdoj.gov/pardon/.

Notes: Clemency statistics include pardons, commutations, and remissions of fines. Figures have been rounded to the nearest whole number.

Controversial acts of clemency may be among those granted in the final months of an Administration, such as President G. H.W. Bush's pardon of key figures in the Iran-Contra affair on Christmas Eve, 1992—less than four weeks before the end of his term—and President Clinton's pardon of commodities trader Marc Rich, which was issued on President Clinton's last day in office.[110]

Possible Congressional Concerns

Acts of Clemency Might Restrict Oversight of the Executive Branch

Ongoing investigations into the conduct of executive branch officials may be impeded or effectively ended by acts of clemency. As previously noted, President G.H.W. Bush pardoned six former officials from President Reagan's Administration for their roles in the Iran-Contra affair, including two officials who had been indicted but had not yet been to trial. These pardons essentially ended the Independent Counsel's criminal investigation, which had begun six years earlier.

Acts of Clemency Might Have Implications for U.S. Foreign Relations

In one of his last acts before leaving office, President G.W. Bush commuted the sentences of two U.S. Border Patrol agents convicted of shooting a Mexican citizen who had crossed illegally into Texas. The government of Mexico, which has been highly critical of what it deems "the excessive use of force" by American border authorities, was opposed to any clemency for the agents.[111] Mexico's assistant foreign minister for North American affairs criticized the commutation, describing it as "a very bad and difficult to understand message" that appeared to put "demands by anti-immigrant groups" ahead of "the efforts of the Mexican government."[112] It has also been suggested President G.W. Bush, prior to leaving office, considered clemency for soldiers convicted of crimes committed while serving at Abu Ghraib prison in Iraq.[113]

---

[110] Eric Lichtblau and Davan Maharaj, "Clinton Pardon of Rich a Saga of Power, Money and Influence," *Los Angeles Times*, February 18, 2001, at http://articles.latimes.com/2001/feb/18/news/mn-27173.

[111] "Mexico Slams Border Shooting, US Congress for Failing to Pass Immigration Bill," *New York Times*, Global Edition, August 9, 2008, at http://www.iht.com/articles/ap/2007/08/10/america/LA-GEN-Mexico-Immigration.php.

[112] Todd J. Gillman and Laura Isenee, "Bush Commutes Sentences of Border Patrol Agents," *Dallas Morning News*, January 20, 2009, at http://www.dallasnews.com/sharedcontent/dws/news/world/mexico/stories/012009dnnatborder.cb9616f.html.

[113] Keith Koffler, "Stevens Case Puts Spotlight on Pardons," *Roll Call Newspaper Online*, October 28, 2008, at http://www.rollcall.com/news/29610-1.html.

Cybersecurity Issues[114]

The increasing importance of maintaining U.S. cybersecurity has made it a critical element of the nation's broader national security apparatus. The 2015 National Security Strategy highlights "cyber" as a "shared space" (akin to oceans, air, and space) and an element of national security.[115] Additionally, the Director of National Intelligence (DNI) included an assessment of cyberspace-based threats in the 2016 *Worldwide Threat Assessment of the US Intelligence Community.*[116]

Although cybersecurity is an ongoing concern, the presidential transition period may present its own set of challenges in this area. Cybersecurity concerns may be heightened if a cybersecurity incident occurs during the transition, or positions (including PAS and non-PAS) with cybersecurity responsibilities are not filled in a timely manner.

Cybersecurity Incident Coordination

An architecture that allows federal agencies to coordinate their responsibilities for cybersecurity incidents is vital to the federal government's capability to prepare for, respond to, or recover from a cybersecurity incident. On July 26, 2016, President Obama released Presidential Policy Directive 41 (PPD-41), "United States Cyber Incident Coordination," which provides a unifying architecture for a coordinated cyber incident response among federal departments and agencies.[117]

PPD-41 establishes incident response principles which are shared by the victim entity and any entity which may assist them (whether a private security firm or federal agency). When responding to an incident, federal government agencies are to be guided by the following principles: (1) the relevant federal agencies, private sector, and individuals share responsibility for responding to the incident; (2) the federal government's response is to be based on a risk assessment; (3) the federal government is to safeguard incident details, privacy, civil liberties, and sensitive information, to the extent permitted by law; (4) the federal government's response is to be unified; and (5) the federal response is to be carried out in a way that facilitates the recovery and restoration of the entity that experienced the incident.[118]

The directive also establishes federal agency lines of effort and the lead agency for each line of effort.

- *Threat Response* includes activities related to law enforcement and national security investigations to gather evidence and identify the actor(s) responsible for the incident. The Department of Justice (DOJ), acting through the Federal Bureau

---

[114] Prepared by (name redacted), Analyst in Cybersecurity Policy, Government and Finance Division.

[115] The White House, *National Security Strategy*, Washington, DC, February 2015, https://www.whitehouse.gov/sites/default/files/docs/2015_national_security_strategy.pdf.

[116] U.S. Congress, Senate Committee on Armed Services, *Worldwide Threat Assessment of the US Intelligence Community*, Statement for the Record, prepared by James R. Clapper, Director of National Intelligence, 114th Cong., 2nd sess., February 9, 2016, at https://www.dni.gov/files/documents/SASC_Unclassified_2016_ATA_SFR_FINAL.pdf.

[117] U.S. President (Obama), Presidential Policy Directive 41,"United States Cyber Incident Coordination," July 26, 2016, at https://www.whitehouse.gov/the-press-office/2016/07/26/presidential-policy-directive-united-states-cyber-incident; U.S. President (Obama), Annex for PPD-41, United States Cyber Incident Coordination, "Federal Government Coordination Architecture for Significant Cyber Incidents," July 26, 2016, at https://www.whitehouse.gov/the-press-office/2016/07/26/annex-presidential-policy-directive-united-states-cyber-incident.

[118] Obama, Presidential Policy Directive 41,"United States Cyber Incident Coordination."

of Investigation (FBI) and the National Cyber Investigative Joint Task Force (NCIJTF), is the government lead for this line of effort.
- *Asset Response* includes providing technical assistance to the victim entity to mitigate the impacts of the incident and restore functionality. The Department of Homeland Security (DHS), acting through the National Cybersecurity and Communications Integration Center (NCCIC), is the federal lead for this line of effort.
- *Intelligence Support* includes activities related to intelligence collection in support of threat and asset response activities and analysis. The Office of the Director of National Intelligence (ODNI), acting through the Cyber Threat Intelligence Integration Center (CTIIC), is the federal lead for this line of effort.

The Department of Defense (DOD) does not have the lead for a line of effort, but it is identified as the lead for the Defense Industrial Base critical infrastructure sector and is required to participate in national response planning.

Although the stated aim of this policy is to help stakeholder communities understand how the U.S. government will respond to a cybersecurity incident, it does not discuss the allocation of agencies' responsibilities. Specifically, PPD-41 does not address the matter of agencies' unique responsibilities and shared (or overlapping) responsibilities for cybersecurity beyond the duration of time when agencies are responding to an incident.

The intelligence community (IC) provides an intelligence briefing to each party's presidential candidate. The topics and issues covered in these briefings reportedly align with the Director of National Intelligence's "Worldwide Threat Assessment" report to Congress.[119] The Worldwide Threat Assessment for 2016 began with a discussion of cybersecurity and technology threats, to include challenges presented by the Internet of Things, artificial intelligence, integrity of information, infrastructure weaknesses, targeting of personally identifiable information, and deterrence in cyberspace.[120] The assessment also identified Russia, China, Iran, North Korea, and nonstate actors as the greatest threat actors in cyberspace.[121]

Positions with Cybersecurity Responsibilities

Another possible issue involves the cybersecurity qualifications of executive branch political appointees, particularly agency heads, and the implications for the federal government and the nation, if some positions are not filled in a timely manner.[122]

Some agency heads, such as the Secretaries of Defense and Homeland Security, lead organizations that have cybersecurity missions. However, all federal agency heads have a cybersecurity responsibility for their agencies' systems, data, and networks. Per the Federal Information Security Management Act (FISMA; P.L. 113-283), each agency head is responsible for

---

[119] Justin Fischel, "Classified Intelligence Briefings For Presidential Candidates: Questions Answered," *ABC News*, August 5, 2016, at http://abcnews.go.com/Politics/classified-intelligence-briefings-presidential-candidates-questions-answered/story?id=41145433.

[120] Clapper, *Worldwide Threat Assessment of the US Intelligence Community*, statement for the record.

[121] Ibid.

[122] CRS Report R44083, *Appointment and Confirmation of Executive Branch Leadership: An Overview*, by (name redacted) and (name redacted).

providing information security protections commensurate with the risk and magnitude of the harm resulting from unauthorized access, use, disclosure, disruption, modification, or destruction of information collected or maintained by or on behalf of the agency; and information systems used or operated by an agency or by a contractor of an agency or other organization on behalf of an agency.[123]

In recent years, Congress has included agency heads in hearings over cybersecurity incidents. For example, in April 2016, the Senate Finance Committee included the Commissioner of the Internal Revenue Service (IRS) on a panel during a hearing on cybersecurity.[124] Because of their overarching managerial responsibilities (namely, with budget and resource prioritization), agency heads have cybersecurity responsibilities incumbent in their positions, regardless of the overall agency's cybersecurity roles and responsibilities.

Other cybersecurity responsibilities may belong to other officials within federal agencies. Chief Information Security Officers (CISOs) have explicit responsibilities for the security of an agency's information technology in the Clinger-Cohen Act of 1996 and the Federal Information Technology Acquisition Reform Act (FITARA).[125]

In the event a nationally significant cybersecurity incident occurs while one or more cybersecurity positions are vacant, the possible implications are unknown. Agencies are responsible for planning for vacancies and devolving responsibilities to career employees.[126] Furthermore, PPD-41 establishes a Cyber Response Group (CRG) to coordinate national policy and a Cyber Unified Coordination Group (Cyber UCG) to coordinate national operations. Through these coordination mechanisms, federal agencies would have an opportunity to become aware of key vacancies and adjust their policy or operational responses accordingly.[127]

National Security Considerations and Options[128]

A presidential transition period[129] is a unique time in America and holds the promise of opportunity, as well as a possible risk to the nation's security interests. While changes in Administration during U.S. involvement in national security-related activities are not unique to the 2016-2017 election period, many observers suggest that the current security environment may portend a time of increased risk. Whether the enemies of the United States choose to undertake action that may harm the nation's security interests during the 2016-2017 election transition period, or the new President experiences a relatively peaceful period during the transition, many foreign policy and security challenges will await the new Administration. Collaboration and

---

[123] 44 U.S.C. §3554.

[124] U.S. Congress, Senate Committee on Finance, *Cybersecurity and Protecting Taxpayer Information*, 114th Cong., 2nd sess., April 12, 2016.

[125] The Clinger-Cohen Act, otherwise known as the Information Technology Management Reform Act of 1996, was included in the National Defense Authorization Act of 1996, P.L. 104-106. FITARA is P.L. 113-291.

[126] 3 U.S.C. §102 note; PTA, §4(f)(2).

[127] U.S. President (Obama), Presidential Policy Directive 41,"United States Cyber Incident Coordination"; U.S. President (Obama), Annex for PPD-41, United States Cyber Incident Coordination, "Federal Government Coordination Architecture for Significant Cyber Incidents."

[128] Prepared by (name redacted), Specialist in Terrorism and National Security, Foreign Affairs, Defense and Trade Division. For a thorough explanation of national security considerations and options during presidential transitions, see CRS Report R42773, *2012-2013 Presidential Election Period: National Security Considerations and Options*, by (name redacted) .

[129] The presidential *election* period encompasses all pre- and post-election day transition-related issues and activities whereas the presidential *transition* period ranges from the day of the election to the inauguration.

coordination during the presidential election period between the current Administration and the new one may have a long-lasting effect on the new President's ability to effectively safeguard U.S. interests and may affect the legacy of the outgoing President.

On a given day the outgoing Administration has the ability to change the policies of a nation and possibly affect the international security environment, yet the following day the President and the national security leadership team may be replaced by a new set of leaders who could have different strategy and policy goals.[130] This political dynamic, coupled with the inherent uncertainty accompanying a presidential transfer of power, may provide an opportunity for those who wish to harm U.S. security interests. Unlike other man-made incidents that may occur with little warning, the presidential transition period offers a broadly defined time frame in which an enemy of the United States may decide to undertake an incident of national security significance[131] in an attempt to manipulate the nation's foreign and domestic policies.[132]

Risks Accompanying the Presidential Transition Period

Many national security observers speculate that extremist groups and some foreign powers might prefer to take action just prior to or after election day. However, the timing of such acts may be solely based on the convergence of an entity attaining a desired capability with a perceived best opportunity to successfully complete its objective. Furthermore, an attack or event that occurs at any time during the presidential transition period could affect the transition and the Administration's policies.[133]

Presidential Transition Period Considerations

Many presidential historians argue that, during the early days of a new Administration, decisionmaking activities will, in part, be based on information provided by the outgoing Administration. Specifically, some scholars state that "enhanced cooperation and communication between the two Administrations is demanded by national security and foreign policy

---

[130] William P. Marshall and Jack M. Beermann, "The Law of Presidential Transitions," Boston University School of Law Working Paper No. 05-15, 2005, pp. 1 - 2. "The outgoing President retains all the formal legal powers of the presidency, yet his last electoral success is four years removed and his political capital is at low ebb.... [H]e may also affirmatively want to create obstacles to prevent his successor from too quickly achieving political and policy success." Ibid. "The incoming president, on the other hand, will be focused on beginning her own initiatives and ... may desire to expeditiously reverse the policies of the previous president." Ibid., p. 2. "When the two Presidents are from opposing parties, the conflicts during the transition period, certainly, will be even more acute." Ibid.

[131] While an "incident of national security significance" could entail a catastrophic natural disaster, this term, for purposes of this report, is used to describe foreign and domestic security-related man-made acts, including a terrorist attack (in the United States, against interests overseas, or against an ally), significant offensive action against troops deployed overseas, assassination of a U.S. or foreign leader, seizure or attacking of an embassy or consulate, a change in the political environment where the United States is undertaking stabilization activities, significant foreign power nuclear-related activity, or a foreign power or extremist group taking military action against a U.S. ally.

[132] Transitions in American government power are not reserved for the executive branch. Congressional elections and changes in state and local leadership are also occasions where individuals wishing to harm U.S. national security interests could place the nation at risk. While the focus of this section is on security implications during a presidential transition, it is acknowledged that planning, prevention, preparedness, response, and recovery activities could also be hampered should an incident of national security concern occur during a congressional or nonfederal government election period.

[133] For example, while the terrorist attacks of March 2004 did appear to have an effect on the election outcome and the Spanish government's support of military actions in Iraq, the new prime minister actually increased Spain's commitment to counterterrorism military efforts in Afghanistan. It is speculated that while the tactical operation may have been a success, the long-term results of the attack were counter to the strategic desires of the terrorist group.

concerns."[134] It is further observed that, "as the world becomes more dangerous and the risks to harm more immediate, the need for effective and seamless transitions becomes correspondingly greater."[135]

To further complicate matters, modern presidential transition activities are no longer constrained to the time between the election and inauguration.[136] Some presidential historians argue that, "history tells us that any winning candidate who has not started [transition efforts] at least six months before the election will be woefully behind come the day after the election day."[137] While the exact time period and phases of a presidential transition are not statutorily or constitutionally defined, the presidential transition period could be seen as comprising five phases, extending from presidential campaign activities to the new President's establishment of a national security team and development of accompanying strategies and policies.[138]

Congressional and Executive Branch Options

The executive branch is not alone in attempting to ensure the country passes power from one Administration to the next in a safe and thoughtful manner.[139] However, the outgoing and incoming Administrations are viewed as being primarily responsible for addressing risks to the nation and taking actions to prevent and respond to any incident that may affect transition-related processes. How the newly elected President recognizes and responds to these challenges will "depend heavily upon the planning and learning that takes place during the transition from one Administration to another."[140] During past presidential transitions, the current and incoming Administrations and Congress have traditionally undertaken numerous activities to facilitate a smooth transfer of executive branch power. Some of the actions often taken during presidential transitions include

- consulting with government and private sector experts who have presidential transition expertise,
- providing information to the President-elect after the election and prior to the inauguration,
- offering operational briefings on ongoing national security matters to prospective presidential nominees and their staff,

---

[134] Todd J. Zywicki, "The Law of Presidential Transitions and the 2000 Election," *Brigham Young University Law Review*, vol. 1573, 2001, p.1.

[135] Ibid; Marshall and Beermann, "The Law of Presidential Transitions," p. 9.

[136] Glenn P. Hastedt and Anthony J. Eksterowicz, "Perils of Presidential Transition," *Seton Hall Journal of Diplomacy and International Relations,* vol. II, no. 1, Winter/Spring 2001, p. 67.

[137] John Kamensky, "One Year and Counting," IBM Center for The Business of Government Weblog, November 6, 2007, at https://transition2008.wordpress.com/2007/11/06/one-year-and-counting/.

[138] For a complete explanation of the five phases of the presidential transition period and accompanying national security considerations, see CRS Report R42773, *2012-2013 Presidential Election Period: National Security Considerations and Options*, by (name redacted).

[139] Congress and state and local governments provide support to various aspects of the presidential transition. Other government and nongovernmental entities that offer advice and assistance to presidential transition related activities include the General Services Administration, National Archives and Records Administration, Office of Government Ethics, Congressional Research Service, Government Accountability Office, Center for the Study of the Presidency, Council for Excellence in Government, Mandate for Leadership Project, Presidential Appointment Initiative, Reason Public Policy Institute, and the Transition to Governing Project.

[140] Hastedt and Eksterowicz, "Perils of Presidential Transition," p. 67.

- preparing briefing books and policy memos detailing the issues of most concern to the current Administration, and
- expediting security clearances for President-elect transition team members.

Agency Rulemaking[141]

When Congress enacts a statute, it often delegates rulemaking authority to one or more federal agencies to implement the statute. Agencies are required to follow certain procedures when they issue those rules. For example, under the Administrative Procedure Act (APA), agencies are generally required to publish a notice of rulemaking in the *Federal Register*, take comments on the proposed rule, and publish a final rule in the *Federal Register*.[142] Because regulations carry the force of law and may have significant policy effects, they are an important policymaking tool for the federal government and for a presidential Administration.

Overview of Midnight Rulemaking

During the final months of recent presidential Administrations, federal agencies have issued an increased number of regulations.[143] This phenomenon is often referred to as "midnight rulemaking." Various scholars and public officials have documented evidence of midnight rulemaking by several recent outgoing Administrations, especially for those outgoing Administrations that will be replaced by an Administration of a different party.[144]

One general concern raised about midnight rulemaking is that an outgoing Administration may have less political accountability compared to an Administration faced with the possibility of reelection, and that agencies may not have sufficient time to review and digest public comments taken during the comment period.[145] Another concern is that the quality of the regulations may suffer during the midnight period, because the departing Administration may issue rules quickly, and, as a result, the rules may not receive adequate review within the agency itself or from the Office of Management and Budget (OMB).[146] Finally, some have argued that the task of

---

[141] Prepared by (name redacted), Specialist in Government Organization and Management, Government and Finance Division.

[142] The APA is at 5 U.S.C. §551 *et seq*. For additional information on the rulemaking process, see CRS Report RL32240, *The Federal Rulemaking Process: An Overview*, coordinated by (name redacted).

[143] See CRS Report R42612, *Midnight Rulemaking: Background and Options for Congress*, by (name redacted).

[144] See, for example, Anne Joseph O'Connell, "Agency Rulemaking and Political Transitions," *Northwestern University Law Review*, vol. 105, no. 2 (2011), pp. 471-534; Anne Joseph O'Connell, "Political Cycles of Rulemaking: An Empirical Portrait of the Modern Administrative State," *Virginia Law Review*, vol. 94, no. 4 (June 2008), pp. 889-986.; and Patrick A. McLaughlin, "The Consequences of Midnight Regulations and Other Surges in Regulatory Activity," *Public Choice*, vol. 147, no. 3/4 (June 2011), pp. 395-412.

[145] Jack M. Beermann, "Midnight Rules: A Reform Agenda," draft report prepared for the consideration of the Administrative Conference of the United States, March 3, 2012, at http://www.acus.gov/wp-content/uploads/downloads/2012/03/Revised-Draft-Midnight-Rules-Report-3-13-12.pdf. Beermann cited an example in which an agency had to review 300,000 comments in one week to issue a rule on time.

[146] Under Executive Order 12866, OMB's Office of Information and Regulatory Affairs (OIRA) reviews most agencies' significant rules before they are published in the *Federal Register*, both at the proposed rule stage and final rule stage. This includes a review of the rule itself and the agency's cost-benefit analysis of the rule, if one is required. See Executive Order 12866, "Regulatory Planning and Review," 58 *Federal Register* 51735, October 4, 1993. For more information about OIRA's role in this process, see CRS Report RL32397, *Federal Rulemaking: The Role of the Office of Information and Regulatory Affairs*, coordinated by (name redacted).

evaluating a previous Administration's midnight rules can potentially overwhelm a new Administration.[147]

On the other hand, a 2012 study for the Administrative Conference of the United States (ACUS) concluded that many midnight regulations were "relatively routine matters not implicating new policy initiatives by incumbent administrations," and that the "majority of the rules appear to be the result of finishing tasks that were initiated before the Presidential transition period or the result of deadlines outside the agency's control (such as year-end statutory or court-ordered deadlines)."[148]

Regulatory Moratoria and Postponements

One approach previous Presidents have used to control rulemaking at the start of their Administrations has been the imposition of a moratorium on new regulations from executive departments and independent agencies. Such moratoria have sometimes been accompanied by a requirement that the departments and agencies postpone the effective dates of certain rules that were issued at the end of the previous President's term.[149] Also, any proposed rules that have not been published in the *Federal Register* as final rules by the time the outgoing President leaves office can be withdrawn by a new Administration. However, once final rules have been published in the *Federal Register*, the only way for a new Administration to eliminate or change them is to go through the rulemaking process again.[150]

A few weeks after he took office in 1981, President Reagan issued Executive Order 12291, which, among other things, generally required covered agencies to "suspend or postpone the effective dates of all major rules that they have promulgated in final form as of the date of this Order, but that have not yet become effective."[151] In 1993, the incoming Clinton Administration imposed a moratorium on rules issued at the end of the G. H.W. Bush Administration.[152] Similarly, on January 20, 2001, the incoming G. W. Bush Administration issued a memorandum delaying the implementation of many rules issued in the last months of the Clinton Administration.[153] Most recently, on January 20, 2009, Rahm Emanuel, then-assistant to President Obama and chief of staff, sent a memorandum to the heads of executive departments and agencies requesting that they generally (1) not send proposed or final rules to the Office of the Federal Register, (2) withdraw from the Office rules that had not yet been published in the *Federal Register*, and (3) consider postponing for 60 days the effective dates of rules that had been published in the *Federal Register* but had not yet taken effect.[154]

---

[147] See, for example, the testimony of Michael Abramowicz, U.S. Congress, House Committee on the Judiciary, Subcommittee on Commercial and Administrative Law, *Midnight Rulemaking: Shedding Some Light*, 111th Cong., 1st sess., February 4, 2009, H. Hrg. 111-2 (Washington: GPO, 2009), pp. 236-242.

[148] Beermann, "Midnight Rules," pp. 1-2.

[149] Such presidential moratoria on rulemaking have generally exempted regulations issued by independent regulatory boards and commissions, as well as regulations issued in response to emergency situations or statutory or judicial deadlines.

[150] Under the APA, "rulemaking" is defined as "formulating, amending, or repealing a rule," meaning that an agency must follow the rulemaking procedures set forth by the APA to change or repeal a rule (5 U.S.C. §551(5)). Such procedures apply even for a change to a rule's effective date.

[151] Executive Order 12291, "Federal Regulation," 46 *Federal Register* 13193, February 17, 1981.

[152] U.S. Office of Management and Budget, "Regulatory Review," 58 *Federal Register* 6074, January 22, 1993.

[153] Executive Office of the President, "Memorandum for the Heads and Acting Heads of Executive Departments and Agencies," 66 *Federal Register* 7702, January 24, 2001.

[154] Executive Office of the President, "Memorandum for the Heads of Executive Departments and Agencies," 74 (continued...)

Recent outgoing Administrations have attempted to protect rules issued in their final months from the possibility of being rendered ineffective by establishing an effective date prior to the advent of the new Administration. For example, President G. W. Bush's Chief of Staff, Joshua B. Bolten, issued a memorandum encouraging agencies to issue their proposed rules no later than June 1, 2008, and final regulations no later than November 1, 2008.[155] Similarly, on December 17, 2015, President Obama's OIRA Administrator, Howard Shelanski, wrote a memorandum to deputy secretaries asking them to "strive to complete their highest priority rulemakings by the summer of 2016 to avoid an end-of-year scramble that has the potential to lower the quality of regulations that OIRA receives for review and to tax the resources available for interagency review."[156]

Options for Congress: Oversight of Midnight Rules

Congress may examine the issuance of proposed and final midnight regulations at the end of an Administration and conclude that they should be allowed to go forward. Should Congress conclude otherwise, though, various options are available—even for rules that have already taken effect. First, Congress can use its legislative power to overturn or change a regulation that has been issued by an agency. Congress can also use its legislative power to amend the statutory authority underlying a regulation. A change in the underlying statutory authority could force an agency to amend a regulation that has already been issued, or it could provide additional instruction to an agency while a rule is under development and before it has been finalized.

In addition, Congress may use the expedited procedures provided in the Congressional Review Act (CRA) to disapprove agency rules, including, in some cases, rules issued during a previous session of Congress and by the previous Administration. Alternatively, Congress can add provisions to agency appropriations bills to prohibit certain rules from being implemented or enforced. These two options are discussed in detail below.

Congressional Review Act[157]

Congress may use its general legislative powers to overturn agency rules by regular legislation. The CRA, enacted in 1996, was an attempt by Congress to reassert control over agency rulemaking by establishing a special set of expedited or "fast track" legislative procedures for this purpose, primarily in the Senate.[158]

In short, the CRA requires that all final rules (including rules issued by independent boards and commissions) be submitted to both houses of Congress and to the Government Accountability Office (GAO) before they can take effect. Members of Congress have 60 "days of continuous

---

(...continued)

Federal Register 4435, January 26, 2009.

[155] Memorandum from Joshua B. Bolten, White House Chief of Staff, to Heads of Executive Departments and Agencies, May 9, 2008.

[156] Memorandum from Howard Shelanski, Administrator, Office of Information and Regulatory Affairs, to Deputy Secretaries, December 17, 2015.

[157] For an overview of the CRA, see CRS Report R43992, *The Congressional Review Act (CRA): Frequently Asked Questions*, by (name redacted) and (name redacted).

[158] The following discussion is a synopsis of more detailed information provided in other CRS reports. For a detailed discussion of CRA disapproval procedures, see CRS Report RL31160, *Disapproval of Regulations by Congress: Procedure Under the Congressional Review Act*, by (name redacted). For a discussion of the "carryover" procedures, see CRS Report RL34633, *Congressional Review Act: Disapproval of Rules in a Subsequent Session of Congress*, by (name redacted) and (name redacted).

session" to introduce a joint resolution of disapproval beginning on the date a rule has been received by Congress (hereinafter referred to as the "initiation period").[159] The Senate has 60 "session days" from the date the rule is received by Congress and published in the *Federal Register* to use expedited procedures to act on a resolution of disapproval (hereinafter referred to as the "action period").[160] For example, once a joint resolution has reached the floor of the Senate, the CRA makes consideration of the measure privileged, prohibits various other dilatory actions, disallows amendments, and limits floor debate to a maximum of 10 hours. If passed by both houses of Congress, the joint resolution is then presented to the President for signature or veto. If the President signs the resolution, the CRA specifies not only that the rule "shall not take effect" (or shall not continue if it has already taken effect), but also that the rule may not be reissued in "substantially the same form" without subsequent statutory authorization.[161] Also, the act states that any rule disapproved through these procedures "shall be treated as though such rule had never taken effect."[162] If, on the other hand, the President vetoes the joint resolution, then (as is the case with any other bill) Congress can override the President's veto by a two-thirds vote in both houses of Congress.

Under most circumstances, it is likely that the President would veto such a resolution in order to protect rules developed under his own Administration, and it may also be difficult for Congress to muster the two-thirds vote in both houses needed to overturn the veto. Of the over 71,000 final rules that have been submitted to Congress since the legislation was enacted in 1996, the CRA has been used to disapprove one rule—the Occupational Safety and Health Administration's November 2000 final rule on ergonomics.[163] The March 2001 rejection of the ergonomics rule was the result of a specific set of circumstances created by a transition in party control of the presidency. Because of the structure of the periods during which Congress can take action under the CRA, there may be a period at the beginning of each new Administration during which rules issued near the end of the previous Administration would be eligible for consideration under the CRA. Such a period is often considered the most likely time in which Congress would be able to overturn a rule successfully using the CRA.

Appropriations Provisions

Along with one use of the CRA to overturn an agency rule, Congress has frequently added provisions to agency appropriations bills to affect rulemaking and regulations, and Congress could choose to apply such provisions to midnight rules. Frequently, such provisions prohibit the use of funds for certain rulemaking-related purposes.[164] This could include, for example,

---

[159] "Days of continuous session" excludes all days when either the House of Representatives or the Senate is adjourned for more than three days, that is, pursuant to an adjournment resolution.

[160] "Session days" include only calendar days on which a chamber is in session. Once introduced, resolutions of disapproval are referred to the committees of jurisdiction in each house of Congress. The House of Representatives would consider the resolution under its general procedures, likely as prescribed by a special rule reported from the Committee on Rules. In the Senate, however, if the committee has not reported a disapproval resolution within 20 calendar days after the regulation has been submitted and published in the *Federal Register*, then the committee may be discharged and the resolution placed on the Senate calendar if 30 Senators submit a petition to do so.

[161] 5 U.S.C. §801(b)(2).

[162] 5 U.S.C. §801(f).

[163] U.S. Department of Labor, Occupational Safety and Health Administration, "Ergonomics Program," 65 *Federal Register* 68261, November 14, 2000. Although the CRA has been used to disapprove only one rule, it may have other, less direct or discernable effects (e.g., keeping Congress informed about agency rulemaking and preventing the publication of rules that may be disapproved).

[164] Provisions in appropriations acts that affect rulemaking may also require agencies to take certain actions. For (continued...)

prohibitions on the use of funds for the development or finalization of proposed or final rules, or prohibitions on the use of funds for implementation or enforcement of rules that have already been finalized.

Restrictions on the use of funds in appropriations bills can enable Congress to have a substantial effect on agency rulemaking and regulatory activity beyond the introduction of joint resolutions of disapproval pursuant to the CRA. However, unlike CRA joint resolutions of disapproval, these types of appropriations provisions do not nullify the force or effect of an existing regulation.[165] Therefore, any final rule that has taken effect and been codified in the *Code of Federal Regulations* will continue to be binding—even if language in the relevant regulatory agency's appropriations act prohibits the use of funds to enforce the rule. Regulated entities are still required to adhere to applicable requirements (e.g., installation of pollution control devices, submission of relevant paperwork), even if violations are unlikely to be detected and enforcement actions cannot be taken by federal agencies.

There may be additional limits on the ability to influence agency rulemaking through restrictions on the use of funds. For example, restrictions on the use of funds in appropriations acts, unless otherwise specified, are binding only for the period of time covered by the measure (i.e., a fiscal year or a portion of a fiscal year).[166] The provisions are generally applicable only to the agencies funded by that appropriations measure, unless otherwise specified. Some provisions are worded to affect agencies that are funded in other appropriations bills (e.g., those that prohibit the use of funds in "this or any other Act"), or they may be designated as "general provisions" that are "government-wide" and therefore are applicable to virtually all federal agencies.[167] In addition, some federal regulatory agencies derive a substantial amount of their operating funds from sources other than congressional appropriations (e.g., user fees), and the use of those funds to develop, implement, or enforce rules may not be legally constrained by language preventing the use of appropriated funds.[168] Finally, when federal regulations are primarily implemented or enforced by state or local governments (e.g., many of those issued by the Environmental Protection Agency and the Occupational Safety and Health Administration), those governments

---

(...continued)

example, agencies may be directed to develop rules in particular areas or enforce existing rules in particular ways. This section does not discuss these types of provisions. For general information on appropriations restrictions, see CRS Report R41634, *Limitations in Appropriations Measures: An Overview of Procedural Issues*, by (name redacted) and (name redacted) .

[165] Provisions have been included in appropriations acts that directly affect the substance of existing or future regulations, but these are not drafted as funding prohibitions.

[166] See GAO, *Principles of Appropriations Law, Third Edition, Volume I*, GAO-04-261SP, January 2004, p. 2-34, which states that, "Since an appropriation act is made for a particular fiscal year, the starting presumption is that everything contained in the act is effective only for the fiscal year covered. Thus, the rule is: A provision contained in an annual appropriation act is not to be construed to be permanent legislation unless the language used therein or the nature of the provision makes it clear that Congress intended it to be permanent."

[167] See GAO, *Principles of Appropriations Law*, p. 2-33, which says that a general provision "may apply solely to the act in which it is contained ('No part of any appropriation contained in this Act shall be used ...'), or it may have general applicability ('No part of any appropriation contained in this or any other Act shall be used ...')." For example, for FY2012, Title VII of Division C of the Consolidated Appropriations Act was designated as "General Provisions—Government-Wide."

[168] Others, however, take the view that even these nonappropriated funds must be at least figuratively deposited into the Treasury, and that "all spending in the name of the United States must be pursuant to legislative appropriation." Kate Stith, "Congress' Power of the Purse," *The Yale Law Journal*, vol. 97 (1988), p. 1345.

may have sources of funding that are independent of the federal funds that can be restricted by the appropriations provisions.[169]

Executive Branch Political Appointments into the Next Presidency[170]

The installation of executive branch political appointees is another area of presidential activity that may be of concern to Congress in the last months of an Administration. Under certain circumstances, outgoing Presidents have used the constitutional authority of the office to make recess appointments that extended into the succeeding presidency.

Appointment Authority for Officers of the United States

In general, the President and the Senate share the power to fill the top nonelected offices of the U.S. government. As part of its system of checks and balances, the Constitution provides a general framework for appointments to these positions:

> [The President] shall nominate, and by and with the Advice and Consent of the Senate, shall appoint Ambassadors, other public Ministers and Consuls, Judges of the supreme Court, and all other Officers of the United States, whose Appointments are not herein otherwise provided for, and which shall be established by Law: but the Congress may by Law vest the Appointment of such inferior Officers, as they think proper, in the President alone, in the Courts of Law, or in the Heads of Departments.[171]

In practice, the appointment process has three phases: (1) the President selects, vets, and nominates an individual, with or without input from Senators; (2) the Senate considers the nomination, with or without further action; and (3) if the nomination is confirmed by the Senate, the President signs a commission, and the appointee is sworn in.[172]

The Constitution also empowers the President unilaterally to make a temporary appointment to such a position if it is vacant and the Senate is in recess.[173] Such an appointment, termed a recess appointment, expires at the end of the following session of the Senate.[174] At the longest, a recess appointment made in early January, after the beginning of a new session of the Senate, would last until the Senate adjourns sine die at the end of the following year, a period that could be nearly two years in duration.

Developments over the last decade have decreased the likelihood that a departing President could install a Senate-opposed appointee using the recess appointment power, particularly where one or

---

[169] See GAO, *Principles of Federal Appropriations Law, Third Edition, Volume II*, GAO-06-382, February 2006, which says that, unless stated otherwise, expenditures by recipients of federal grants "are not subject to all the same restrictions and limitations imposed on direct expenditures by the federal government. For this reason, grant funds in the hands of a grantee have been said to largely lose their character and identity as federal funds."

[170] Prepared by (name redacted), Specialist in American National Government, Government and Finance Division.

[171] Art. II, §2, cl. 2.

[172] For detailed information about the appointment process, see CRS Report R44083, *Appointment and Confirmation of Executive Branch Leadership: An Overview*, by (name redacted) and (name redacted); and CRS Report RL31980, *Senate Consideration of Presidential Nominations: Committee and Floor Procedure*, by (name redacted) .

[173] Article 2, §2, clause 3 reads, "The President shall have Power to fill up all Vacancies that may happen during the Recess of the Senate, by granting Commissions which shall expire at the End of their next Session."

[174] Each Congress covers a two-year period, generally composed of two sessions.

both chambers are led by the party in opposition to the President. From the 110th Congress onward, it has become common for the Senate and House to use certain scheduling practices as a means of precluding the President from making recess appointments.[175] The practices do this by preventing the occurrence of a Senate recess of sufficient length for the President to be able to use his recess appointment authority. In a June 26, 2014, opinion, the U.S. Supreme Court held that the President's recess appointment power may be used only during a recess of 10 days or longer except under "some very unusual circumstance."[176]

Tenure during a Transition for a Confirmed Appointee

Unless otherwise specified in law, appointees to executive branch positions usually serve at the pleasure of the President. That is, they serve for an indeterminate period of time and can be removed by the President at any time for any reason (or no stated reason).[177] By tradition, appointees to these positions usually step down when the appointing President leaves office, unless asked to stay by the President-elect.

Congress has periodically elected to set a specific term of office for a particular position, restrict the President's power of removal for a particular position, or both. Some removal restriction provisions require only that the President inform Congress of his reasons for removing an official, while others require that a certain threshold, such as "neglect of duty, or malfeasance in office, or for other good cause shown," be met.[178] The use of fixed terms and removal restrictions has been more common for positions on regulatory and other boards and commissions, for which Congress has elected to establish a greater level of independence from the President, than for positions in executive departments and single-headed agencies.[179] An appointee to a position with a fixed term and protection from removal may serve during more than one presidency and is not required to step down when the appointing President leaves office; the incoming President may not remove the appointee unless the grounds for such removal would meet the threshold established in statute. An appointee to a position with a fixed term but no specified protection from removal may be protected from removal nonetheless, based on case law.[180] Even where an appointee to

---

[175] The evolution of this use of scheduling practices is discussed in greater detail in CRS Report R42329, *Recess Appointments Made by President Barack Obama*, by (name redacted).

[176] Nat'l Labor Relations Bd. v. Noel Canning, 134 S. Ct. 2550, at 2567 (2014). The opinion gave as an example of an unusual circumstance an instance such as "a national catastrophe ... that renders the Senate unavailable but calls for an urgent response" and further noted that "political opposition in the Senate would not qualify as an unusual circumstance."

[177] It has long been recognized that "the power of removal [is] incident to the power of appointment." (*Ex Parte Hennen*, 38 U.S. (13 Pet.) 230, 259 (1839).)

[178] There appears to be no standard clarifying under what circumstances the thresholds set by these statutory terms regarding removal might be met. (See Marshall J. Breger and Gary J. Edles, "Established by Practice: The Theory and Operation of Independent Federal Agencies," *Administrative Law Review*, vol. 52 (2000), p. 1111, at pp. 1144-1145.) A Senate committee has asserted, however, that a removal for good cause must be based on "some type of misconduct," as opposed to the refusal to carry out a presidential order. (See U.S. Congress, Senate Committee on Governmental Affairs, *Independent Counsel Reauthorization Act of 1987*, report to accompany S. 1293, 100th Cong., 1st sess., S.Rept. 100-123 (Washington: GPO, 1987), pp. 12-13.)

[179] Although fixed terms and removal protections for department and single-headed agency positions are unusual, notable examples do exist. The position of Commissioner of Social Security, for example, has a six-year term, and "[a]n individual serving in the office of Commissioner may be removed from office only pursuant to a finding by the President of neglect of duty or malfeasance in office." (42 U.S.C. §902(a).) Similar provisions are associated with leaders of the Office of Special Counsel (5 U.S.C. §1211), the Federal Housing Finance Agency (12 U.S.C. §4512), and the Consumer Financial Protection Bureau (12 U.S.C. §5491).

[180] See, for example, *S.E.C. v. Blinder, Robinson & Co., Inc.*, 855 F.2d 677, 681 (10th Cir. 1988), in which the Court of (continued...)

such a position is not protected from removal, it could be argued that the fixed term establishes the expectation that the incumbent will be able to serve for a certain period. Removal of such an appointee by the incoming President might entail an expenditure of political capital.

Tenure during a Transition for a Recess Appointee

At times in the past, outgoing Presidents have made recess appointments, during their final months in office, to each of the kinds of positions described above. The potential tenure for recess appointees to positions without removal protections is the same as it would be if the appointee had been confirmed by the Senate; they typically leave with the appointing President. Recess appointees to positions with fixed terms and removal protection, however, may serve until the expiration of the term to which they were appointed or the expiration of the recess appointment, whichever occurs earlier.[181] A President could, at the end of his presidency, use a recess appointment to bypass the Senate and fill a fixed-term position for a period that would outlast his time in office by a year or more. As noted above, even an appointee without explicit statutory removal protection might prove difficult or costly for an incoming President to remove.

In some cases, recess appointees who serve past the end of an Administration might be "consensus appointees," who have the support of the incoming President and the reconstituted Senate. In other cases, however, an outgoing President could install more controversial appointees, who would not be nominated by the new President or confirmed by the reconstituted Senate to the positions to which they are appointed. As previously noted, developments over the last decade have decreased the likelihood that a departing President could install a Senate-opposed appointee using the recess appointment power, particularly where one or both chambers are led by the party in opposition to the President.

Notwithstanding the low likelihood of a late-term recess appointment by the President within the current context,[182] arguments could be advanced in support of, and opposition to, the practice. In support, it could be argued that the outgoing President carries the full constitutional authority of the office until his term is over, that he must be able to exercise that authority as he sees fit, and that he should not be expected to abstain from implementing his agenda until he leaves office. Furthermore, it might be argued, other recent Presidents have made recess appointments in their final months in office, and some of these recess appointments have been to positions with terms that carry over into the following Presidency. A counter argument might be made that, in making recess appointments to fixed term positions with removal protections, an outgoing President would be effectively circumventing the Senate and undermining the incoming President.

(...continued)

Appeals for the Tenth Circuit stated that "it is commonly understood that the President may remove a commissioner only for 'inefficiency, neglect of duty or malfeasance in office.'"

[181] As previously noted, a recess appointment can last for as much as nearly two years. A full fixed term is usually of longer duration, but sometimes individuals are appointed to the final portion of an unexpired term that is already under way (e.g., the final year of a five-year term begun by another appointee).

[182] Floor remarks by one Senator in early 2016 suggest that the majority intends, for the duration of President Obama's time in office, to follow scheduling practices that would appear to preclude a recess of sufficient length to allow him to make a recess appointment. Senator James Lankford, "Comprehensive Addiction and Recovery Act of 2015," remarks in the Senate, *Congressional Record*, daily edition, vol. 162, part 38 (March 9, 2016), p. S1359.

Judicial Branch Appointments[183]

As with executive branch political appointees, the procedure for appointing federal judges is provided for by the Constitution in a few words. The Appointments Clause (Article II, Section 2, clause 2) states that the President "shall nominate, and by and with the Advice and Consent of the Senate, shall appoint ... Judges of the supreme Court, and all other Officers of the United States," including lower federal court judges (i.e., U.S. circuit and district court judges).[184]

The appointment process for federal judges is similar to that of executive branch appointees in that the President is responsible for submitting a nomination to the Senate (which, in turn, may or may not act on the nomination). While the process of appointing federal judges has undergone some changes over two centuries, its most essential feature—the sharing of power between the President and the Senate[185]—has remained unchanged: To receive appointment as a federal judge, one must first be formally selected ("nominated") by the President[186] and then approved ("confirmed") by the Senate.[187]

Vacancies Awaiting a New President

At the onset of a new Administration, there are typically dozens of vacant lower federal court judgeships awaiting nominations by a new President.[188] It is, however, relatively rare for a vacancy on the Supreme Court to exist at the start of a new presidency. At present, there is a vacancy on the Court that may not be filled prior to a new President assuming office on January 20, 2017.[189]

---

[183] Prepared by (name redacted), Analyst in American National Government, Government and Finance Division.

[184] The focus of this section is on vacant U.S. circuit and district court judgeships. Additionally, this section does not address vacancies on the U.S. Court of International Trade (a specialized court with nine authorized judgeships).

[185] One of the primary ways in which the Senate exercises its power in the judicial appointment process is through the "blue slip" procedure of the Judiciary Committee, a procedure which affords Senators the opportunity to convey to the President their views about candidates under consideration for judgeships in their states. In recent and many past Congresses, the Judiciary Committee's blue slip procedure has reinforced Senators' influence over judicial nominations in their state by permitting nominations to receive committee action only when both home state Senators have returned "positive" blue slips. Note that, generally, Senators exert less influence over a President's selection of circuit court nominees than they do over his selection of district court nominees.

[186] A president may also make a recess appointment to a vacant U.S. circuit or district court judgeships. Such recess appointments, however, are relatively rare.

[187] The most common ways in which a judicial nomination fails to receive Senate confirmation include (1) the full Senate voting against the confirmation; (2) the President withdrawing the nomination because the Senate Judiciary Committee has voted against reporting the nomination to the Senate or has made clear its intention not to act on the nomination, or because the nomination, even if reported, is likely to face substantial opposition on the Senate floor, or because the nominee has requested that the nomination be withdrawn; and (3) the Senate, without confirming or rejecting the nomination, returning the nomination to the President under Rule XXXI, paragraph 6 of the *Standing Rules of the Senate* after it has adjourned or been in recess for more than 30 days.

[188] At the end of a Congress that coincides with the end of a presidency, the Senate typically returns any outstanding judicial nominations to the outgoing President (who does not then re-nominate individuals prior to leaving office on January 20). A relatively recent exception to this was during the final weeks of the Clinton presidency. The Senate, under the provisions of Senate Rule XXXI, paragraph 6 of the Standing Rules of the Senate, returned a number of circuit court nominations to the President in December 2000 at the conclusion of the 106th Congress. At the beginning of the 107th Congress, in January 2001, President Clinton resubmitted 9 of these nominations to the Senate prior to leaving office several weeks later on January 20. The nominations were eventually withdrawn by President G.W. Bush in March 2001.

[189] The current vacancy was created by the death of Antonin Scalia on February 13, 2016. As of this writing, Majority (continued...)

The relatively large number of vacant judgeships at the beginning of a new presidency is due, in part, to the Senate approving fewer judicial nominations during an outgoing President's final year in office (particularly if it is a President's eighth year in office).[190] Additionally, the Senate typically has not approved U.S. circuit court nominations during a presidential election year past June or July of the election year, regardless of whether it is the fourth or eighth year of a presidency.[191]

Beginning with President Ronald Reagan, the number of vacant circuit court judgeships[192] on January 20 of a newly elected President's first year in office included 5 (1981); 10 for the George H.W. Bush presidency (1989); 18 for the Clinton presidency (1993); 26 for the George W. Bush presidency (2001); and 13 for the Obama presidency (2009).

The number of vacant district court judgeships[193] on January 20 of a newly elected President's first year in office included 29 at the start of the Reagan presidency (1981); 27 for the George H.W. Bush presidency (1989); 93 for the Clinton presidency (1993); 55 for the George W. Bush presidency (2001); and 45 for the Obama presidency (2009).

Timing of Nominations Made by a New President

Prior to a President nominating an individual to a lower federal court judgeship, there can be a lengthy pre-nomination evaluation of judicial candidates by staff in the White House Counsel's Office, as well as by the Department of Justice. Candidate finalists also undergo a confidential background investigation by the Federal Bureau of Investigation (FBI) and an independent evaluation by a committee of the American Bar Association. The selection process is completed when the President, approving of a particular candidate, signs a nomination message (which is then transmitted to the Senate).[194]

Given the steps involved in the pre-nomination stage, it is often at least several months before the Administration submits its first circuit and district court nominations to the Senate for consideration. During the Reagan presidency, the first circuit court nomination was submitted on

---

(...continued)

Leader Mitch McConnell (R-KY) has stated that the Scalia vacancy will not be filled until after President Obama's successor takes office. Senator Mitch McConnell, Press Release, "McConnell On Supreme Court Nomination," March 16, 2016, at http://www.mcconnell.senate.gov/public/index.cfm?p=PressReleases&ContentRecord_id=50492600-6758-4FC2-928D-302FAB54BEA8. Additionally, for further discussion of a President's selection of a nominee for the Supreme Court, see CRS Report R44235, *Supreme Court Appointment Process: President's Selection of a Nominee*, by (name redacted) .

[190] For further discussion, see CRS Report R44353, *Final Senate Action on U.S. Circuit and District Court Nominations During a President's Eighth Year in Office*, by (name redacted) .

[191] For example, in 2012, the last circuit court nomination approved by the Senate during the calendar year was on June 12 (while the last district court nomination was approved during the lame duck session in December). In 2008, the last circuit court nomination approved by the Senate during the calendar year was on June 24 (while the last district court nomination was approved on September 26). In 2004, the last circuit court nomination approved during the calendar year was similarly on June 24 (while the last district court nomination was approved during the lame duck session in November). For further discussion of the processing of judicial nominations by the Senate during presidential election years, see CRS Report R42600, *Confirmation of U.S. Circuit and District Court Nominations in Presidential Election Years*, by (name redacted) and (name redacted) .

[192] U.S. circuit courts take appeals from U.S. district courts and are also empowered to review the decisions of many administrative agencies.

[193] U.S. district courts are the federal trial courts of general jurisdiction.

[194] For further discussion, see CRS Report R43762, *The Appointment Process for U.S. Circuit and District Court Nominations: An Overview*, by (name redacted) .

July 16, 1981. During the G.H.W. Bush, Clinton, and G.W. Bush presidencies, the first circuit court nominations were submitted on February 28, 1989,[195] August 6, 1993, and May 9, 2001, respectively. During President Obama's first year in office, the first circuit court nomination was submitted on March 17, 2009.

Regarding district court nominations, the first nomination was submitted by President Reagan on July 8, 1981. During the G.H.W. Bush, Clinton, and G.W. Bush presidencies, the first district court nominations were submitted on February 28, 1989,[196] August 6, 1993, and May 17, 2001, respectively. During President Obama's first year in office, the first district court nomination was submitted on June 25, 2009.

Executive Orders[197]

Concerns about the volume, timing, and content of executive orders may be heightened during presidential transitions. The perception, if not necessarily the reality, exists that an outgoing President's inclination to act unilaterally increases during the transition period.

Executive orders are a significant vehicle for unilateral action by the President: they have the force and effect of law—unless voided or revoked by congressional, presidential, or judicial action—and they combine "the highest levels of substance, discretion, and direct presidential involvement."[198] Being able to act unilaterally enables a President to establish control over policymaking. Presidents are sometimes aided in this endeavor by the proliferation and ambiguity of statutes, which increase their opportunities for justifying presidential action.[199] Another appealing feature of executive orders is that they allow Presidents to act "quickly, forcefully, and (if they like) with no advance notice."[200] Capitalizing on these features enables Presidents to seize the initiative on an issue, shape the national agenda, and force others to respond. For practical or political reasons, Presidents may choose to use executive orders to circumvent a Congress that they perceive as hostile to their policies, after considering whether the Congress is likely to overturn a particular executive order,[201] or as moving too slowly.[202]

Executive orders suit the needs of an outgoing President who wants to establish or change policy, or is striving to secure his legacy. Howell and Mayer have noted that when a President's

---

[195] President G.H.W. Bush renominated two circuit court nominees who had previously been nominated by President Reagan but whose nominations were not approved by the Senate prior to the end of the 100th Congress. President G.H.W. Bush submitted his third circuit court nomination on August 4, 1989.

[196] President G.H.W. Bush renominated three district court nominees who had been nominated by President Reagan but whose nominations were not approved by the Senate prior to the end of the 100th Congress. President G.H.W. Bush submitted his fourth district court nomination on August 4, 1989.

[197] Prepared by (name redacted), Specialist in American National Government, Government and Finance D ivision.

[198] Joel L. Fleishman and Arthur H. Aufses, "Law and Orders: The Problem of Presidential Legislation," *Law and Contemporary Problems*, vol. 40 (1976), p. 5. Executive orders disposition tables, which list each President's executive orders from Franklin D. Roosevelt through the current President, are at http://www.archives.gov/federal-register/executive-orders/disposition.html.

[199] Terry M. Moe and William J. Howell, "The Presidential Power of Unilateral Action," *Journal of Law, Economics, and Organization*, vol. 15 (1999), pp. 141 and 143.

[200] Ibid., p. 138.

[201] Christopher J. Deering and Forrest Maltzman, "The Politics of Executive Orders: Legislative Constraints on Presidential Power," *Political Research Quarterly*, vol. 52 (1999), pp. 2 and 6.

[202] Paul C. Light, *The President's Agenda: Domestic Policy Choice from Kennedy to Reagan* (Baltimore: Johns Hopkins University Press, 1991), p. 118.

successor belongs to the opposition political party, "he has every reason to hurry through last-minute public policies, doing whatever possible to tie his successor's hands."[203] An outgoing President's use of unilateral directives, such as executive orders, might be greeted with criticism from some quarters. Some scholars note that the "directives lack the sort of legitimacy that pre-election activity has, because by definition they are issued after a president (and, in many cases, his party) has been repudiated at the polls. Moreover, there are no opportunities for democratic accountability, because, again, voters do not have a subsequent chance to express their approval or disapproval."[204]

An incoming President, who is eager to act quickly on his policy agenda, seeking to modify or overturn certain of his predecessor's actions, or distinguish himself from his predecessor, particularly when they are from different parties, would find executive orders an effective way to accomplish these objectives.[205] He might be stymied, though, in his efforts to amend his predecessor's actions: "Occasionally, presidents cannot alter orders set by their predecessors without paying a considerable political price, undermining the nation's credibility, or confronting serious legal obstacles."[206]

Timing and Volume of Executive Orders

Table 2 presents the number of executive orders issued by Presidents Obama, G.W. Bush, Clinton, G.H.W. Bush, Reagan, and Carter in each of three different transition periods.[207] These three periods are comparable, but not equal, in duration, which means it is more meaningful to compare data within each column rather than across columns.

---

[203] Howell and Mayer, "The Last One Hundred Days," p. 533.

[204] Ibid., p. 551.

[205] Kenneth R. Mayer, "Executive Orders and Presidential Power," *Journal of Politics*, vol. 61 (1999), p. 451. For example, President Clinton signed E.O. 12834 on January 20, 1993, which required his senior political appointees to take an ethics pledge that would prohibit them from lobbying federal government officials for five years. President George W. Bush launched a major initiative early in his term with the signing of E.O. 13198 and E.O. 13199 on January 29, 2001, which directed the Attorney General and four cabinets secretaries to establish offices of faith-based and community initiatives, and which established a White House Office of Faith-Based and Community Initiatives, respectively.

[206] Howell and Mayer, "The Last One Hundred Days," p. 543. On the other hand, as the following examples show, several recent Presidents revoked, partly or completely, one or more executive orders issued by their immediate predecessor. President Reagan revoked two executive orders signed by President Carter, thus terminating certain aspects of the government's wage and price program (E.O. 12288, January 29, 1981) and disbanding the Tahoe Federal Coordinating Council (E.O. 12298, March 12, 1981). President Clinton revoked (E.O. 12836, February 1, 1993) two of President Bush's executive orders having to do with labor unions. President G.W. Bush signed four executive orders (Executive Orders 13201, 13202, 13203, and 13204), on February 17, 2001, that dealt with labor issues and that partially or completely revoked executive orders that had been signed by his predecessor.

[207] For the sake of consistency within this report, the 41st President is identified as President George H.W. Bush or President G.H.W. Bush. However, he signed his executive orders as President George Bush or President Bush. His son, the 43rd President, is identified as President George W. Bush (his signature on executive orders) or President G.W. Bush.

Table 2. Number of Executive Orders Issued During Presidential Transitions, 1977-Present

President	Incoming: (First term) Jan. 20-Apr. 30	Pre-election: (Final term) Aug. 1-Election	Lame Duck: (Final term) Election-Jan. 20
Donald J. Trump	33 (2017)	—	—
Barack Obama	10 (2009)	6 (2012) 14 (2016)	17 (2016-2017)
George W. Bush	12 (2001)	10 (2004) 7 (2008)	11 (2008-2009)
William J. Clinton	13 (1993)	10 (1996) 11 (2000)	22 (2000-2001)
George H.W. Bush	11 (1989)	7 (1992)	14 (1992-1993)
Ronald Reagan	18 (1981)	7 (1984) 9 (1988)	12 (1988-1989)
Jimmy Carter	16 (1977)	20 (1980)	36 (1980-1981)

Sources: U.S. National Archives and Records Administration, "Executive Orders Disposition Tables," at http://www.archives.gov/federal-register/executive-orders/disposition.html.

Note: Executive orders are categorized according to signing date.

As incoming Presidents, Obama, G.W. Bush, Clinton, G.H.W. Bush, Reagan, and Carter issued comparable numbers of executive orders. The range of executive orders issued was 10 (Obama) to 18 (Reagan). By signing 33 executive orders during the incoming period, Donald J. Trump nearly doubled the number of orders that were signed by Reagan. During the pre-election period, four of the Presidents also issued comparable numbers of executive orders, ranging from 7 (Reagan, G.H.W. Bush, and G.W. Bush) to 11 (Clinton). President Carter issued 20 executive orders during the pre-election period. The lame duck period shows the greatest variation. Reagan, G.H.W. Bush, G.W. Bush, and Obama each issued fewer than 20 executive orders: 12, 14, 11, and 17, respectively. Clinton issued 22, and Carter issued 36.[208] However, nearly one-third of the

---

[208] The quantity of orders President Carter signed during the pre-election and lame duck periods is consistent with the pace he maintained throughout his four-year term. President Obama issued an average of 32 executive orders per year; President G.W. Bush 36; President Clinton 46; President G.H.W. Bush 42; President Reagan 48; and President Carter 80. The figure for President Obama is an average for the years 2009-2015. National Archives and Records Administration, "Administration of Barack Obama (2009-Present)," at http://www.archives.gov/federal-register/executive-orders/obama.html; National Archives and Records Administration, "Administration of George W. Bush (2001-2009)," at http://www.archives.gov/federal-register/executive-orders/wbush.html; National Archives and Records Administration, "Administration of William J. Clinton (1993-2001)," at http://www.archives.gov/federal-register/executive-orders/clinton.html; National Archives and Records Administration, "Administration of George Bush (1989-1993)," at http://www.archives.gov/federal-register/executive-orders/bush.html; National Archives and (continued...)

executive orders President Carter signed at the end of his term had to do with the hostage crisis in Iran.

A study that examined executive orders issued between April 1936 and December 1995 found that, while the start of a new President's term does not result in a higher number of executive orders, the end of a President's term is notable for an increase in the quantity of executive orders issued.[209] Presidents who were succeeded by a member of the other party signed "nearly six additional orders ... in the last month of their term, nearly double the average level."[210] When party control of the White House did not change following a presidential election, there was "no corresponding increase in order frequency...."[211] The author of this study asserts that these data are evidence that "executive orders have a strong policy component, as otherwise presidents would have little reason to issue such last-minute orders." Mayer also found that reelection plays a role in the number of executive orders signed and issued. Presidents who were running for reelection issued approximately 1.4 more executive orders per month—14 during campaign season from January 1 through the end of October—than when they were not running for reelection.[212]

Content of Executive Orders

Executive orders range, in terms of their import for government management and operations and the principle of shared powers, and the scope of their impact, from the somewhat innocuous to the highly significant. Presidents use executive orders to recognize groups and organizations; establish commissions, task forces, and committees; and make symbolic statements. Presidents also use executive orders "to establish policy, reorganize executive branch agencies, alter administrative and regulatory processes, [and] affect how legislation is interpreted and implemented."[213]

Unilateral action by Presidents during transition periods can, and does, result in a mixture of executive orders in terms of their significance and scope. President Carter established a committee charged with selecting a director for the FBI and closed the federal government on Friday, December 26, 1980.[214] President Bush designated the Organization of Eastern Caribbean States as a public international organization and delegated some disaster relief and emergency assistance functions from the President to the director of the Federal Emergency Management Agency.[215] Turning to executive orders with policy implications, President Reagan brought

---

(...continued)

Records Administration, "Administration of Ronald Reagan (1981-1989)," at http://www.archives.gov/federal-register/executive-orders/reagan.html; National Archives and Records Administration, "Administration of Jimmy Carter (1977-1981)," at http://www.archives.gov/federal-register/executive-orders/carter.html.

[209] Mayer, "Executive Orders and Presidential Power," p. 457.

[210] Ibid.

[211] Ibid.

[212] Ibid., p. 459.

[213] Ibid., p. 445.

[214] Executive Order 11971, "Establishing the Committee on Selection of the Director of the Federal Bureau of Investigation," 42 *Federal Register* 9155, February 15, 1977,.and Executive Order 12255, "Providing for the Closing of Government Departments and Agencies on Friday, December 26, 1980," 45 *Federal Register* 80807, December 5, 1980, respectively.

[215] Executive Order 12669, "Organization of Eastern Caribbean States," 54 *Federal Register* 7753, February 23, 1989, and Executive Order 12673, "Delegation of Disaster Relief and Emergency Assistance Functions," 54 *Federal Register* 12571, March 23, 1989, respectively.

agency rulemaking under the control of OMB and required cost-benefit analyses be conducted for proposed rules.[216] Most notable among the executive orders signed by President Carter during a transition period was a package of executive orders relating to the negotiated release of American hostages being held in Iran.[217]

Submission of the President's Budget in Transition Years[218]

When a new Congress convenes in January, one of its first orders of business is to receive the annual budget submission of the President. Following receipt of the President's budget submission, Congress begins the consideration of the budget resolution and other budgetary legislation for the upcoming fiscal year, which starts on October 1.[219] The transition from one presidential Administration to another raises special issues regarding the annual budget submission. Which President—the outgoing President or the incoming one—is required to submit the budget, and how will the transition affect the timing and form of the submission? This section provides background information that addresses these questions.[220]

Is the Outgoing or Incoming President Required to Submit the Budget?

The Budget and Accounting Act of 1921, as amended, requires the President to submit a budget annually to Congress toward the beginning of each regular session.[221] This requirement first applied to President Warren Harding, for FY1923.

The deadline for submission of the budget, first set in 1921 as "on the first day of each regular session," has changed several times over the years:

- in 1950, to "during the first 15 days of each regular session";[222]

---

[216] Executive Order 12291, "Federal Regulation," 46 *Federal Register* 13193, February 17, 1981.

[217] Executive Order 12276, "Direction Relating to Establishment of Escrow Accounts," 46 *Federal Register* 7913, January 23, 1981; Executive Order 12277, "Direction to Transfer Iranian Government Assets," 46 *Federal Register* 7915, January 23, 1981; Executive Order 12278, "Direction to Transfer Iranian Government Assets Overseas, 46 *Federal Register* 7917, January 23, 1981; Executive Order 12279, "Direction to Transfer Iranian Government Assets Held by Domestic Banks," 46 *Federal Register* 7917, January 23, 1981; Executive Order 12280, "Direction to Transfer Government Financial Assets Held by Non-banking Institutions," 46 *Federal Register* 7921, January 23, 1981; Executive Order 12281, "Direction to Transfer Certain Iranian Government Assets," 46 *Federal Register* 7923, January 23, 1981; Executive Order 12282, "Revocation of Prohibitions Against Transactions Involving Iran," 46 *Federal Register* 7925, January 23, 1981; Executive Order 12283, "Non-prosecution of Claims of Hostages and for Actions at the United States Embassy and Elsewhere," 46 *Federal Register* 7927, January 23, 1981; Executive Order 12284, "Restrictions on the Transfer of Property of the Former Shah of Iran," 46 *Federal Register* 7929, January 23, 1981; Executive Order 12285, "President's Commission on Hostage Compensation," 46 *Federal Register* 7931, January 23, 1981.

[218] Prepared by (name redacted), Analyst in Government Organization and Management, Government and Finance Division.

[219] For more information on the federal budget process, see CRS Report 98-721, *Introduction to the Federal Budget Process*, coordinated by (name redacted) .

[220] For additional information on this topic, see CRS Report RS20752, *Submission of the President's Budget in Transition Years*, by (name redacted) . For information on the executive budget process generally, see CRS Report R42633, *The Executive Budget Process: An Overview*, by (name redacted) .

[221] 31 U.S.C. §1105a; P.L. 67-13; 42 Stat. 20.

- in 1985, to "on or before the first Monday after January 3 of each year (or on or before February 5 in 1986)";[223] and
- in 1990, to "on or after the first Monday in January but not later than the first Monday in February of each year."[224]

The 20th Amendment to the Constitution, ratified in 1933, requires each new Congress to convene on January 3 (unless the date is changed by the enactment of a law) and provides a January 20 beginning date for a President's four-year term of office. Therefore, under the legal framework for the beginning of a new Congress, the beginning of a new President's term, and the deadline for the submission of the budget, all outgoing Presidents prior to the 1990 change were obligated to submit a budget.

The 1990 change in the deadline made it possible for an outgoing President to leave the annual budget submission to his successor, an option which the three outgoing Presidents since then (G.H.W. Bush, Clinton, and G.W. Bush) have chosen. The most recent budget, for FY2017, was submitted by President Obama. If outgoing President Obama chooses the same option as his three predecessors, the submission of the FY2018 budget would be the responsibility of his successor.

Because President G.H.W. Bush chose not to submit a budget for FY1994 (and was not obligated to do so), President Clinton submitted the original budget for FY1994 rather than budget revisions. Similarly, the budget for FY2002 was submitted by the incoming President G.W. Bush, rather than by outgoing President Clinton, and the budget for FY2010 was submitted by incoming President Obama, rather than outgoing President G.W. Bush.

Transition Year Budgets: Deadlines and Timing of Recent Submissions

During the period beginning with the full implementation of the congressional budget process (in FY1977), six presidential transitions of Administration have occurred. During this time, the three outgoing Presidents required to submit a budget (Ford, Carter, and Reagan) did so on or before the statutory deadline. As mentioned above, the three Presidents who were not required to submit an outgoing budget (George H.W. Bush, Bill Clinton, and George W. Bush) chose to leave the budget submission to their respective successors.

In past years, Congress authorized the submission of a budget for a fiscal year after the statutory deadline by enacting a deadline extension in law. For example, the deadlines for submission of the budgets for FY1981, FY1984, and FY1986 were extended from mid-January to late-January or early-February by P.L. 96-186, P.L. 97-469, and P.L. 99-1, respectively. Beginning in the late 1980s, however, several original budgets were submitted late without authorization. For FY1991, the budget was submitted a week after a deadline that already had been extended by law (P.L. 101-228). For FY1989, the budget was submitted 45 days after the deadline without the consideration of any measure granting a deadline extension.

(...continued)

[222] The 1950 change was made by the Budget and Accounting Procedures Act of 1950 (P.L. 81-784; 64 Stat. 832).

[223] The 1985 change was made by the Balanced Budget and Emergency Deficit Control Act (P.L. 99-177; 99 Stat. 1038).

[224] The 1990 change was made by the Budget Enforcement Act of 1990, which was included in the Omnibus Budget Reconciliation Act of 1990 (P.L. 101-508, Title XIII; 104 Stat. 1388-1573).

The three most recent transition-year budgets (FY1994, FY2002, and FY2010), were submitted 66, 63, and 98 days after the deadline, respectively, without consideration of a measure granting a deadline extension. Presidents Clinton and G.W. Bush submitted the original budgets for FY1994 and FY2002 (on April 8, 1993, and April 9, 2001, respectively). President Obama submitted an overview of his budget, "A New Era of Responsibility: Renewing America's Promise" on February 26, 2009, two days after delivering an address on his economic and budget plan to a joint session of Congress. He submitted his *Appendix*, which contained detailed budget information on May 7, 2009, and additional supplemental volumes, including the *Analytical Perspectives* and the *Terminations, Reductions, and Savings* volume, on May 11, 2009.

Transition Year Budgets: Special Messages and Budget Revisions

Although Presidents Reagan, Clinton, G.W. Bush, and Obama did not submit detailed budget proposals until April or May of their first year in office, each of them advised Congress regarding the general contours of their economic and budgetary policies in special messages transmitted to Congress in February. In addition, each incoming President since Reagan has presented his special message on the budget to a joint session of Congress.[225]

Once the original budget for a fiscal year has been submitted, a President or his successor may submit revisions at any time. Since 1921, incoming Presidents, except for Warren Harding,[226] Clinton, G.W. Bush, and Obama, assumed their position with a budget of their predecessor in place. Six incoming Presidents chose to modify their predecessor's budget by submitting revisions shortly after taking office: Eisenhower, Kennedy, Nixon, Ford, Carter, and Reagan. Six incoming Presidents chose not to submit revisions: Calvin Coolidge, Herbert Hoover, Franklin D. Roosevelt, Truman, Johnson, and G.H.W. Bush.[227]

Since FY1977, two incoming Presidents (Carter[228] and Reagan)[229] submitted revisions of their predecessors' budgets. Though President George H.W. Bush did not submit an official revision of President Reagan's FY1990 budget, he submitted a document to Congress to coincide with his first State of the Union Address that contained many of the same elements as budget revisions that had been submitted by previous incoming Presidents.[230]

---

[225] While not technically State of the Union Addresses, these presentations contain many of the same elements and serve much the same purpose as the State of the Union. As such, they are frequently counted as State of the Union Addresses by scholars. For additional information, see CRS Report R40132, *The President's State of the Union Address: Tradition, Function, and Policy Implications*, by (name redacted) .

[226] Warren G. Harding was the first President required to submit a consolidated federal budget to Congress. For additional information, see CRS Report R43163, *The President's Budget: Overview of Structure and Timing of Submission to Congress*, by (name redacted) .

[227] Presidents Coolidge and Hoover each assumed office with a reduced opportunity of time to submit budget revisions. President Coolidge assumed office on August 3, 1923, following the death of President Harding, which effectively prevented him from submitting budget revisions prior to the start of the fiscal year in July. President Hoover was the final President elected prior to the ratification of the Twentieth Amendment in 1933. Consequently, his term did not begin until March.

[228] The budget revisions are transmitted along with a short Presidential Message, which is noted in the *Congressional Record*. Presidential Message, *Congressional Record*, vol. 123, part 4 (February 22, 1977).

[229] President Reagan submitted two budget revisions for FY1982. See Presidential Message, *Congressional Record*, vol. 127, part 3 (March 10, 1981), p. 3928, and Presidential Message, *Congressional Record*, vol. 127, part 5 (April 7, 1981), p. 6627.

[230] President G.H.W. Bush submitted a 193-page document titled *Building a Better America* to Congress which contained select modifications of the FY1990 budget as well as legislative proposals to reform the budget process. See Presidential Message, *Congressional Record*, vol. 135, part 2 (February 9, 1989), p. 2081.

Appendix. Electoral Vote Allocation by States and the District of Columbia

Figure A-1. Map of State Electoral Vote Allocations, Presidential Elections of 2012, 2016, and 2020

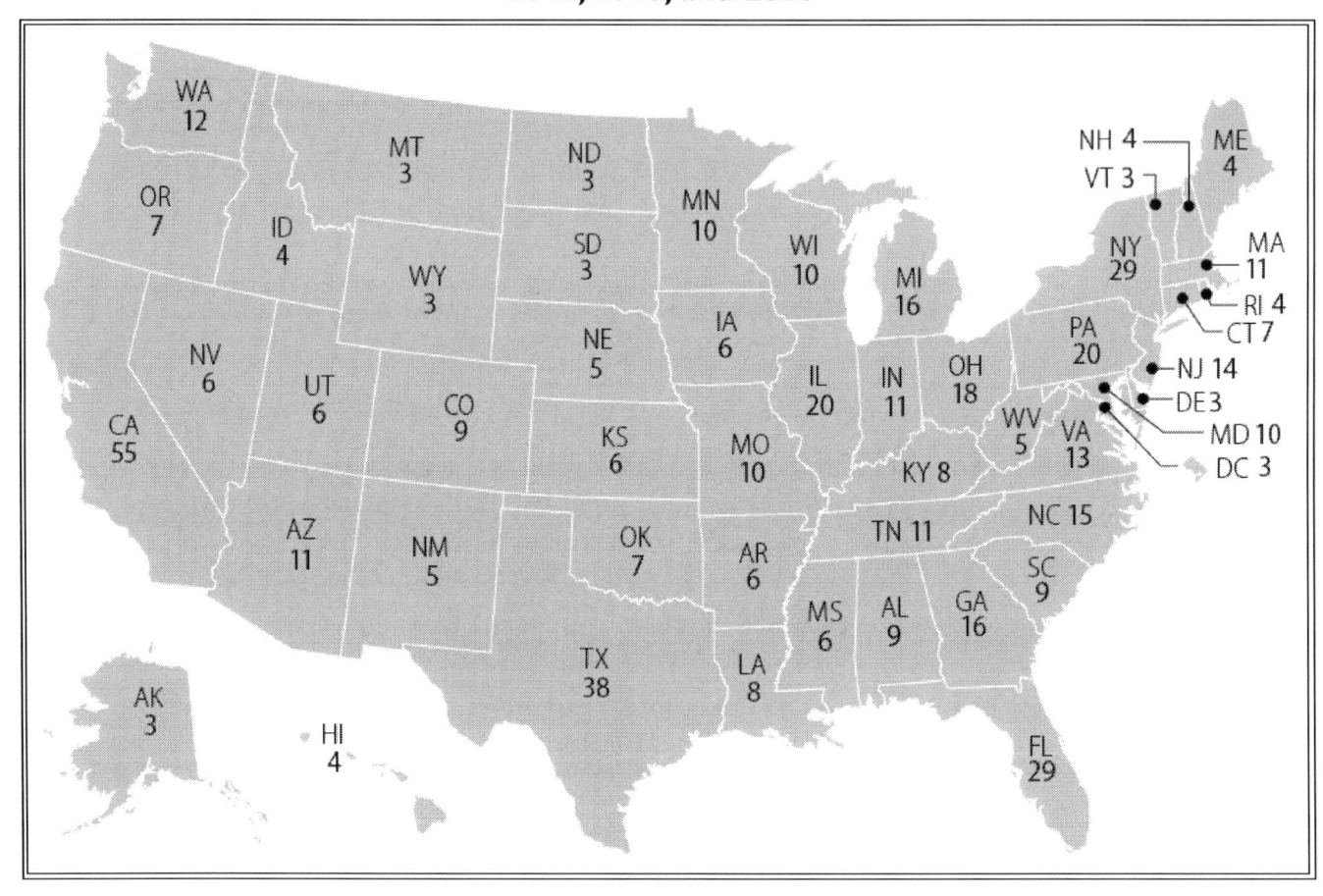

State	EV	State	EV	State	EV
WA	12	NH	4	ME	4
OR	7	VT	3	MA	11
MT	3	NY	29	RI	4
ND	3	CT	7	NJ	14
MN	10	DE	3	MD	10
ID	4	PA	20	DC	3
SD	3	WI	10	MI	16
WY	3	IA	6	IL	20
NE	5	IN	11	OH	18
NV	6	UT	6	CO	9
KS	6	MO	10	WV	5
VA	13	KY	8	TN	11
NC	15	CA	55	AZ	11
NM	5	OK	7	AR	6
MS	6	AL	9	GA	16
SC	9	TX	38	LA	8
AK	3	HI	4	FL	29

Source: Compiled by the Congressional Research Service

From Election to Inauguration—An Overview of the Process

Table A-1. Electoral Vote Allocation by States and the District of Columbia, Presidential Elections of 2012, 2016, and 2020

State	Electors	State	Electors	State	Electors
Alabama	9	Kentucky	8	North Dakota	3
Alaska	3	Louisiana	8	Ohio	18
Arizona	11	Maine	4	Oklahoma	7
Arkansas	6	Maryland	10	Oregon	7
California	55	Massachusetts	11	Pennsylvania	20
Colorado	9	Michigan	16	Rhode Island	4
Connecticut	7	Minnesota	10	South Carolina	9
Delaware	3	Mississippi	6	South Dakota	3
District of Columbia	3	Missouri	10	Tennessee	11
Florida	29	Montana	3	Texas	38
Georgia	16	Nebraska	5	Utah	6
Hawaii	4	Nevada	6	Vermont	3
Idaho	4	New Hampshire	4	Virginia	13
Illinois	20	New Jersey	14	Washington	12
Indiana	11	New Mexico	5	West Virginia	5
Iowa	6	New York	29	Wisconsin	10
Kansas	6	North Carolina	15	Wyoming	3

Source: Compiled by the Congressional Research Service.

Federal Election Results: Frequently Asked Questions

October 8, 2020

R46565

Several states have implemented new election administration processes in response to the COVID-19 pandemic that could affect how and when ballots are counted. Even under normal circumstances, finalizing federal election results takes days or weeks after election day. Among other steps, state, territorial, and local election officials *canvass* votes to ensure that ballots are valid and counted accurately. Election observers, audits, and other processes are designed to enhance transparency. This report addresses frequently asked questions on these and related subjects. The discussion emphasizes the period between the time a voter casts a ballot and when election officials *certify*, or finalize, the results.

Introduction

The results voters see reported on election night are the culmination of several steps in the election administration process, but are not the end of the process. Each state, territory, and the District of Columbia—which administer federal elections—has its own process for counting votes and declaring winners, but all follow similar steps. Election administrators, political officials, and members of the public continue working after election night to finalize official results. This process typically takes several days or even weeks. State- or territorial-level federal election results in the United States are never official on election night. Amid the COVID-19 pandemic in 2020, the additional time required to process far more mail ballots than most jurisdictions normally receive led to slower ballot processing times in some primary elections, and is expected to do so again in the November general election.

The current environment also creates the potential for foreign or domestic disinformation campaigns designed to undermine confidence in American elections as the normal counting process occurs amid greater public scrutiny than that process typically receives. On September 22, 2020, the Federal Bureau of Investigation (FBI) and the Department of Homeland Security's (DHS's) Cybersecurity and Infrastructure Security Agency (CISA) jointly issued a public service announcement noting that "Foreign actors and cybercriminals could exploit the time required to certify and announce elections' results by disseminating disinformation that includes reports of voter suppression, cyberattacks targeting election infrastructure, voter or ballot fraud, and other problems intended to convince the public of the elections' illegitimacy."[1]

These circumstances have generated renewed interest among some Members of Congress, other public officials, and voters about how election officials count votes and determine election results. This report provides brief answers to frequently asked questions about the processes for counting, documenting, and ensuring transparency after votes are cast. It addresses federal elections, although the discussion herein also generally applies to elections for state or local offices.

Professional election administrators manage most or all of the ballot-counting process.[2] Members of the public, the media, or credentialed observers typically monitor most or all of the ballot-counting process.[3] Specific practices and requirements vary by jurisdiction. Election officials develop standard practices to document the chain of custody for ballots, ensure transparency, and generate accurate results.

Scope of the Report

The frequently asked questions below are designed to provide a resource for Members of Congress and congressional staff as they conduct oversight and consider legislation related to

---

[1] Federal Bureau of Investigation and Cybersecurity and Infrastructure Security Agency, Department of Homeland Security, *Foreign Actors and Cybercriminals Likely to Spread Disinformation Regarding 2020 Election Results*, public service announcement I-092220-PSA, September 22, 2020, https://www.ic3.gov/media/2020/200922.aspx.

[2] For a recent profile, see, for example, Natalie Adona et al., *Stewards of Democracy: The Views of American Local Election Officials*, Democracy Fund, report, June 26, 2019, https://democracyfund.org/idea/stewards-of-democracy-the-views-of-american-local-election-officials/.

[3] National Conference of State Legislatures, *Policies for Election Observers*, October 12, 2016, at https://www.ncsl.org/research/elections-and-campaigns/policies-for-election-observers.aspx; and National Conference of State Legislatures, *Post-Election Audits*, October 25, 2019, at https://www.ncsl.org/research/elections-and-campaigns/post-election-audits635926066.aspx.

federal elections. The discussion emphasizes the period between when voters cast ballots and election officials certify election results for federal elections. Because states, territories, and localities administer federal elections, the report contains general discussion of law, policy, and practice in those jurisdictions, but does not attempt to do so comprehensively.[4] The report briefly discusses recounts and contested elections, but those topics are largely beyond the scope of this report. Other CRS products provide information on related topics concerning contested U.S. House elections,[5] the electoral college,[6] and the congressional role in verifying and counting presidential election results.[7]

The report is intentionally brief to make the content more accessible. It does not discuss legislation or identify specific requirements and processes in individual jurisdictions.[8] As such, the general information presented in this report does not assess any election jurisdiction's processes for or performance at administering elections. Similarly, the report does not provide specific compliance information, legal analysis, or policy analysis about critical infrastructure issues. Other CRS reports provide additional information about elections policy issues generally.[9]

---

[4] Federal law typically has relatively little effect on the process of counting and finalizing election results. As noted elsewhere in this report, other CRS products provide additional information about federal and constitutional provisions regarding contests, recounts, and certifying electoral college results.

[5] See CRS Report RL33780, *Procedures for Contested Election Cases in the House of Representatives*, by L. Paige Whitaker.

[6] See, for example, CRS In Focus IF11641, *The Electoral College: A 2020 Presidential Election Timeline*, by Thomas H. Neale; CRS Report R43824, *Electoral College Reform: Contemporary Issues for Congress*, by Thomas H. Neale; and CRS Report R40504, *Contingent Election of the President and Vice President by Congress: Perspectives and Contemporary Analysis*, by Thomas H. Neale.

[7] See CRS Report RL32717, *Counting Electoral Votes: An Overview of Procedures at the Joint Session, Including Objections by Members of Congress*, coordinated by Elizabeth Rybicki and L. Paige Whitaker.

[8] For additional information on the general processes discussed in this report, see, for example, Joint COVID Working Group; Cybersecurity and Infrastructure Security Agency [CISA], Elections Infrastructure Government Coordinating Council, Sector Coordinating Council, *Inbound Ballot Process*, Version 1.0. These and related documents are available on the CISA "#PROTECT2020" website, "Election Security GCC and SCC Resources" section, https://www.cisa.gov/protect2020. See also Tim Harper, Rachel Orey, and Collier Fernekes, *Counting the Vote During the 2020 Election*, Bipartisan Policy Center, August 2020, https://bipartisanpolicy.org/report/counting-the-vote-during-the-2020-election/.

[9] Congressional readers may contact the coauthors of this report for additional information on elections policy. See, for example, CRS Report R45302, *Federal Role in U.S. Campaigns and Elections: An Overview*, by R. Sam Garrett; CRS Report R45549, *The State and Local Role in Election Administration: Duties and Structures*, by Karen L. Shanton; CRS Report R46146, *Campaign and Election Security Policy: Overview and Recent Developments for Congress*, coordinated by R. Sam Garrett; CRS Report R46455, *COVID-19 and Other Election Emergencies: Frequently Asked Questions and Recent Policy Developments*, coordinated by R. Sam Garrett; CRS In Focus IF11477, *Early Voting and Mail Voting: Overview & Issues for Congress*, by Sarah J. Eckman and Karen L. Shanton; and CRS In Focus IF11286, *Election Security: Federal Funding for Securing Election Systems*, by Karen L. Shanton.

From Election to Inauguration—An Overview of the Process   85

> **Brief Background: Ballot Submission to Election Results**
>
> Election jurisdictions around the country use various processes and terminology to count ballots and obtain election results. The information noted below is generally applicable and abbreviated. Additional detail appears in the questions and answers in the text of this report. State, territorial, and local election jurisdictions document and publicize their individual requirements.
>
> - *Submitting Ballots.* Voters deposit completed (also called "marked") ballots in a ballot box or scanner at in-person polling places. Mail and early in-person ballots are received at designated sites across a precinct or at a central location.
> - *Tabulating Ballots.* Ballots are counted, or *tabulated,* where they are cast, at centralized election offices, or both. These tabulations may occur multiple times to verify the accuracy of the total ballot count.
> - *Canvassing Ballots.* Election officials aggregate ballot totals and document and reconcile questions about ballot validity through a process known as *the canvass.*
> - *Certifying Results.* Final election results are called *certified* results. State-level certification occurs after the canvass (and, if required in that state, after audits).
>
> As discussed in the questions and answers in the text of this report, a combination of professional election administrators, volunteers, and members of the public may be involved in these steps, depending on jurisdiction. Documenting chain of custody for ballots, following established procedures for observing elections and challenging ballots, and auditing results also help ensure transparency and accuracy.

What is the difference between returns reported on election night and final results?

Federal election results at the state or territorial levels are never official in the United States until after election day. Results appearing in media reports or that election jurisdictions release on election night are unofficial and preliminary. These initially reported (either by the media or election officials) totals do not necessarily include all ballots submitted in the jurisdiction, have not been subject to the canvassing process, and could change. Consequently, in 2020 and before, it is normal and expected that final election totals differ from those announced on election night. It is also common that the candidates in various races can trade leads throughout election night and after, as additional ballots are counted.[10] Typically, it takes several days or weeks to finalize election results through the canvass (and audits, where applicable) and certify a winner. State or territorial law sets deadlines for how and when these processes occur.

How do states finalize election results?

Although individual procedures vary by state, finalizing election results typically involves two major steps, the *canvass* and *certification*. The *canvass* involves assembling and verifying all validly cast ballots so that they can be aggregated into the final official election results (generally called *certified* results).[11] As an Election Assistance Commission publication explains, "The

---

[10] See, for example, Nathaniel Persily and Charles Stewart III, "Actually, We'll Know a Lot on Election Night," *The Wall Street Journal*, September 26, 2020, p. C4.

[11] For example, the U.S. Election Assistance Commission *Voluntary Voting System Guidelines* define the canvass as a "Compilation of election returns and validation of the outcome that forms the basis of the official results by a political subdivision." See U.S. Election Assistance Commission, *Voluntary Voting System Guidelines,* Vol. 1, Version 1.1 (2015), p. A-5.

purpose of the canvass is to account for every ballot cast and ensure that every valid vote cast is included in the election totals. This involves accounting for every absentee ballot, every early voting ballot, every ballot cast on Election Day, every provisional ballot, every challenged ballot, and every overseas and military ballot."[12] Depending on jurisdiction, groups of professional election officials, appointed canvassing boards, or both conduct the canvass.

Typical steps in the canvass include reconciling any discrepancies in the number of ballots issued versus those cast; duplicating damaged ballots that scanners cannot read, documenting that process, and counting the duplicated ballots; if applicable, addressing discrepancies in signatures or cast ballots (e.g., questions about voter intent based on ballot markings); and reconciling the number of ballots cast with the number of voters who voted in person at the polling place.[13] These processes may be repeated multiple times as precincts and vote centers compile their results and balloting information is consolidated at subsequently higher levels of election administration (e.g., precinct, county, and state).

In some jurisdictions, statistical data and written reports accompany the certified results and provide additional information about the canvassing process and how discrepancies were addressed. Similarly, in some cases, the certification is the final step in the canvassing process. In others, the governor or chief state election official (e.g., secretary of state) issues certified results based on information provided in the canvassing authority's final report or meeting.

In some states, very close election margins during the canvass trigger recounts, discussed at the end of this report. Some jurisdictions also conduct *postelection audits*, which are intended to check the accuracy of the election results.[14] These audits involve comparing the results generated by the election system against a sample of paper records of the vote, such as paper ballots or the voter-verifiable paper audit trails generated by direct-recording electronic voting machines.[15]

---

[12] U.S. Election Assistance Commission, *Quick Start Management Guide: Canvassing and Certifying an Election*, October 2008, p. 3. For additional discussion of military and overseas citizen voting, see, for example, CRS In Focus IF11642, *Absentee Voting for Uniformed Services and Overseas Citizens: Roles and Process, In Brief*, by R. Sam Garrett.

[13] See, for example, U.S. Election Assistance Commission, *Quick Start Management Guide: Canvassing and Certifying an Election*, October 2008, pp. 7-9; and U.S. Election Assistance Commission, *Election Management Guidelines*, pp. 133-138. The *Quick Start* document is available on the EAC website at https://www.eac.gov/election-officials/quick-start-guides. The *Election Management Guidelines* document is available on the EAC website at https://www.eac.gov/election_management_resources/election_management_guidelines.aspx.

[14] National Institute of Standards and Technology, *Election Terminology Glossary – Draft*, https://pages.nist.gov/ElectionGlossary/.

[15] Exactly how jurisdictions that use postelection audits conduct them varies, but postelection audits generally can be grouped into two categories: (1) traditional postelection audits, which sample a fixed percentage of voting districts or machines, and (2) risk-limiting audits, which use statistical methods to determine how many districts or machines have to be sampled to achieve a specified level of confidence that the election results are accurate. For more information about postelection audits in general or risk-limiting audits in particular, see National Academies of Sciences, Engineering, and Medicine, *Securing the Vote: Protecting American Democracy*, Washington, DC, 2018, pp. 93-96, https://www.nap.edu/catalog/25120/securing-the-vote-protecting-american-democracy; National Conference of State Legislatures, *Post-Election Audits*, October 25, 2019, at https://www.ncsl.org/research/elections-and-campaigns/post-election-audits635926066.aspx; and Mark Lindeman and Philip B. Stark, "A Gentle Introduction to Risk-Limiting Audits," *IEEE Security and Privacy*, vol. 10, no. 5 (September-October 2012), pp. 42-49.

What procedures might election jurisdictions use to provide transparency and demonstrate that the canvass is conducted correctly?

Election officials work to ensure that the certified election results they provide are generally perceived to be fair, accurate, and legitimate. One way they do so is by having consistent, reliable, and transparent ballot collection and canvass procedures, which are typically established well before the election. To ensure that individual voters can cast their ballots privately and securely, and that those ballots are handled and counted correctly, multiple election administrators and/or public witnesses, representing multiple political parties, generally are involved at various stages of the vote-collecting and -counting processes.

Certain categories of individuals can serve as *election observers*, as defined by state laws; these observers typically include individuals serving on behalf of various political parties and can also include individuals from nonpartisan civic or legal organizations, as well as academics or unaffiliated individuals. States may require potential observers to obtain certain accreditation.[16] An important role for observers under some state laws is monitoring in-person voting on election day for indications of voter coercion, intimidation, or fraud, as well as technological issues and administrative errors or misapplication of election protocols.[17]

States that utilize drop boxes for mail ballots often have video surveillance or trained election staff monitoring the drop box site during voting and have mechanisms in place for ballot retrieval and chain of custody,[18] such as deploying two individuals to collect ballots from each box.[19] Other elements of the voting process, including signature verification for mail ballots, typically also involve multiple individuals.[20]

---

[16] National Conference of State Legislatures, *Policies for Election Observers*, October 12, 2016, at https://www.ncsl.org/research/elections-and-campaigns/policies-for-election-observers.aspx. This CRS report does not address federal election observers or monitors that may be deployed under the Voting Rights Act. For brief additional discussion, see CRS Report R45302, *Federal Role in U.S. Campaigns and Elections: An Overview*, by R. Sam Garrett.

[17] National Conference of State Legislatures, *Poll Watcher Qualifications*, August 6, 2020, at https://www.ncsl.org/research/elections-and-campaigns/poll-watcher-qualifications.aspx. Federal provisions in criminal law, the Voting Rights Act, or both also could be relevant. See for example, CRS Report R45302, *Federal Role in U.S. Campaigns and Elections: An Overview*, by R. Sam Garrett; and CRS Testimony TE10033, *History and Enforcement of the Voting Rights Act of 1965*, by L. Paige Whitaker.

[18] National Conference of State Legislatures, *VOPP: Table 9: Ballot Drop Box Definitions, Design Features, Location and Number*, August 18, 2020, at https://www.ncsl.org/research/elections-and-campaigns/vopp-table-9-ballot-drop-box-definitions-design-features-location-and-number.aspx.

[19] For example, see Arizona Secretary of State's Office, Elections Services Division, *Arizona Elections Procedures Manual*, December 2019, p. 61, at https://azsos.gov/sites/default/files/2019_ELECTIONS_PROCEDURES_MANUAL_APPROVED.pdf; and California Secretary of State, *Vote-by-Mail Ballot Drop Boxes and Vote-by-Mail Drop-Off Locations*, California Code of Regulations Title 2, div. 7, ch. 3, §20137, Ballot Collection Procedures and Chain of Custody, at https://www.sos.ca.gov/administration/regulations/current-regulations/elections/vote-mail-ballot-drop-boxes-and-drop-locations.

[20] For example, see William Janover and Tom Westphal, "Signature Verification and Mail Ballots: Guaranteeing Access While Preserving Integrity—A Case Study of California's Every Vote Counts Act," *Election Law Journal: Rules, Politics, and Policy*, vol. 19, no. 3 (September 2020), p. 329; and "How are Ballots Processed?" articles available from Grand County, Colorado, Clerk & Recorder's Office, *Ballots & Processing*, at https://www.co.grand.co.us/1093/Ballots-Processing.

In many states, canvassing boards and processes include participants who were not directly involved in the administration of the election itself to help provide impartial review.[21] Most states also allow some election observers or members of the media to access certain postelection procedures,[22] such as counting absentee ballots or conducting postelection audits or logic and accuracy tests.[23] Some jurisdictions may also provide a canvass livestream and allow the public to view the process online.[24] Postelection audits may be conducted by an independent audit board, rather than state or local administrators.[25]

What processes help election officials determine voter eligibility and the validity of ballots cast?

State and local election officials use various mechanisms to ensure that only eligible voters cast ballots and that each voter only votes once in an election. The specific processes vary by state and can further vary based on the type of ballot cast (e.g., in-person or by mail).

Election officials primarily use voter registration data to determine whether or not an individual is eligible to vote in a given election, regardless of whether the voter chooses to vote in-person or via a mail (or absentee) ballot.[26] Election officials use state-level voter registration requirements and procedures,[27] as well as verification requirements under the Help America Vote Act of 2002

---

[21] For example, see Florida Supervisors of Elections, *2020 FSASE Canvasing Board Manual*, at https://www.myfloridaelections.com/portals/fsase/2020%20Canv%20Board%20Manual%20FINAL_reduced.pdf; Minnesota Secretary of State, *Canvassing Boards*, at https://www.sos.state.mn.us/elections-voting/how-elections-work/canvassing-boards/; and Washington Secretary of State, *Introduction to County Canvassing Boards*, at https://www.sos.wa.gov/_assets/elections/introduction-to-county-canvassing-boards.pdf.

[22] National Conference of State Legislatures, *Policies for Election Observers*, October 12, 2016, at https://www.ncsl.org/research/elections-and-campaigns/policies-for-election-observers.aspx; Pamela Brown and Jeremy Herb, "Avalanche of Mail Ballots—And Ballot-Watchers—Threatens to Slow Results After Polls Close," CNN Politics, September 15, 2020, at https://www.cnn.com/2020/09/15/politics/voting-ballots-challenge-election/index.html; National Conference of State Legislatures, *Post-Election Audits*, October 25, 2019, at https://www.ncsl.org/research/elections-and-campaigns/post-election-audits635926066.aspx.

[23] Logic and accuracy tests, which are typically conducted prior to an election but may also be conducted after the election in some jurisdictions, are used to check that election equipment is functioning correctly and that it is programmed and calibrated correctly for the current election. They involve running a test deck of ballots through the election equipment and may be conducted by a team of representatives of multiple political parties, open to the public, or both. See, for example, Texas Secretary of State, *Electronic Voting System Procedures*, https://www.sos.texas.gov/elections/laws/electronic-voting-system-procedures.shtml.

[24] For example, see "Live Stream of County Ballot Tabulation Centers," section from Arizona Secretary of State, *Voting Equipment*, at https://azsos.gov/elections/voting-election/voting-equipment; and Montgomery County, Maryland, Board of Elections, *2020 Presidential General Election Ballot Canvass*, at https://www.montgomerycountymd.gov/Elections/2020PrimaryElection/primary-ballot-canvass.html.

[25] National Conference of State Legislatures, *Post-Election Audits*, October 25, 2019, at https://www.ncsl.org/research/elections-and-campaigns/post-election-audits635926066.aspx.

[26] With the exception of North Dakota, all states and territories require individuals to register to vote prior to casting their ballots in federal elections; for more information, see CRS Report R46406, *Voter Registration: Recent Developments and Issues for Congress*; and CRS Report R45030, *Federal Role in Voter Registration: The National Voter Registration Act of 1993 and Subsequent Developments*. North Dakota does maintain a Central Voter File and requires voters to provide identification; see North Dakota Century Code, ch. 16.1-02, at https://www.legis.nd.gov/cencode/t16-1c02.html, and North Dakota Secretary of State, *ID Required for Voting*, at https://vip.sos.nd.gov/IDRequirements.aspx?ptlhPKID=103&ptlPKID=7.

[27] For more information, see National Conference of State Legislators, *Voter List Accuracy*, March 20, 2020, at https://www.ncsl.org/research/elections-and-campaigns/voter-list-accuracy.aspx.

From Election to Inauguration—An Overview of the Process

(HAVA),[28] to confirm a registrant's identity and eligibility to vote, often by comparing information on voter registration applications with other government agency records.

Once a voter is on a state's list of eligible voters, this information is used by election officials to monitor how, and if, voters have received a ballot, to ensure that each eligible voter can cast a vote and that no voter casts multiple ballots in the same election.[29] When voting in-person, *poll books*, or lists of eligible voters, are used by local election administrators to confirm that individuals are currently registered voters and are at the correct voting location for their precinct or election district. *Electronic* (or *e-poll*) *books* are commonly used today and may be able to provide more recently updated voter information or some voter data in real time.[30] In jurisdictions that use centralized vote centers, e-poll books can help election administrators verify that a voter has not previously voted at another location. In addition to identifying voters from poll book records, 35 states also have some form of voter identification requirement in effect for in-person voting during the 2020 election.[31]

In circumstances where voters can vote by mail, some jurisdictions automatically send ballots to voters and others require voters to request a mail ballot.[32] States that automatically send ballots or ballot request forms to voters generally rely upon address information on file in state voter registration records.[33] In the voter records, election administrators typically note which persons have requested and cast absentee ballots. Ballot tracking measures often allow an individual voter to check the status of his or her mail ballot, following it from the time it is sent out by election administrators to when it is returned and cast.[34] These mail ballot tracking measures, in conjunction with in-person voting records, also help election officials to ensure that only a single ballot is counted for each voter; for example, election officials can void a mail ballot if it has not

---

[28] Under HAVA, for example, voter registration applicants must provide a current and valid driver's license number, the last four digits of their Social Security number, or an alternate, unique identifying number assigned by the state for voter registration purposes (52 U.S.C. §21083(a)(5)(A)(i-ii)). HAVA also requires that states coordinate their voter registration lists with state agency records on felony status and state agency records on death (52 U.S.C. §21083(a)(2)(A)(ii)), and directs state DMV officials to enter into agreements with the Social Security Administration and with the chief state election official to verify and match certain voter registration applicant information (52 U.S.C. §21083(a)(5)(B)). HAVA also requires that new voters who submit a voter registration application by mail, and have not previously voted in a federal election in a state, must provide a current and valid photo identification or present "a current utility bill, bank statement, government check, paycheck, or other government document that shows the name and address of the voter," along with their registration application or when they vote for the first time (52 U.S.C. §21083(b)); individuals who fall into this category and are unable to provide documentation when voting for the first time may cast a provisional ballot.

[29] National Conference of State Legislatures, *Double Voting*, September 3, 2020, at https://www.ncsl.org/research/elections-and-campaigns/double-voting.aspx.

[30] National Conference of State Legislatures, *Electronic Poll Books | e-Poll Books*, October 25, 2019, at https://www.ncsl.org/research/elections-and-campaigns/electronic-pollbooks.aspx.

[31] National Conference of State Legislatures, *Voter Identification Requirements | Voter ID Laws*, August 25, 2020, at https://www.ncsl.org/research/elections-and-campaigns/voter-id.aspx.

[32] See Juliette Love, Matt Stevens, and Lazaro Garmio, "Where Americans Can Vote by Mail in the 2020 Elections," *The New York Times*, August 14, 2020, at https://www.nytimes.com/interactive/2020/08/11/us/politics/vote-by-mail-us-states.html; and Kate Rabinowitz and Brittany Renee Mays, "At Least 83% of American Voters Can Cast Ballots by Mail in the Fall," *The Washington Post*, August 20, 2020, at https://www.washingtonpost.com/graphics/2020/politics/vote-by-mail-states/.

[33] If a voter must request a mail ballot, he or she can often provide a different mailing address for ballot delivery.

[34] Jocelyn Grzeszczak, "These Are the States Where You Can Track Your Mail-In Vote," *Newsweek*, August 18, 2020, at https://www.newsweek.com/these-are-states-where-you-can-track-your-mail-vote-1525920.

yet been cast by a voter who decides to vote in-person instead or if officials receive a mail ballot from a voter after he or she has voted in-person.[35]

States employ a number of measures to verify that a mail ballot is completed by the intended voter.[36] Many jurisdictions require voter signatures to accompany completed mail ballots. The voter's signature often accompanies a legal attestation, asserting the voter's identity and eligibility. Election officials, computer software, or both are used to match the signature(s) submitted by the voter to a known signature on file from the voter's registration records or other government agency records, if applicable, via a process known as *signature verification*.[37] If there is a missing, mismatched, or ambiguous signature, some states contact the voter and may provide an opportunity for the voter to correct the issue through processes known as *signature curing*, which may include an affidavit, a copy of additional identification, or both.[38] States may also have requirements for witness signatures or notarization of mail ballots, and voters may need to submit a copy of their photo identification with a mail ballot in certain circumstances.[39] Election officials may also check to ensure that the return address on a mail ballot matches that of the

---

[35] See, for example, California Secretary of State, *Voting at a Polling Place after Applying to Vote by Mail*, at https://www.sos.ca.gov/elections/voting-resources/voting-california/if-you-applied; and "Michigan's Absentee Voting Process," in Michigan Bureau of Elections, *Election Officials' Manual*, November 2019, ch. 6, at http://www.michigan.gov/documents/sos/VI_Michigans_Absentee_Voting_Process_265992_7.pdf. Some jurisdictions may allow a voter who had previously requested a mail ballot to cast a regular in-person ballot. Other jurisdictions may require a voter who had previously requested a mail ballot to cast a provisional ballot in-person, to allow election administrators to confirm that the mail ballot has not been cast; a provisional ballot may be required, for example, if a voter cannot provide the blank mail ballot to officials at the polling site. For additional discussion, see, for example, Associated Press, "States Have Checks in Place to Prevent Voters From Voting Twice," August 26, 2020, at https://apnews.com/article/9308770212, and Nick Corasaniti and Stephanie Saul, "Is Voting Twice a Felony?" *The New York Times*, September 9, 2020, at https://www.nytimes.com/article/voting-twice.html.

[36] Some states may waive certain requirements to make accommodations for individuals with disabilities who need assistance completing their ballots on a case-by-case basis. For further discussion of these issues, see Maggie Astor, "What It's Like to Vote With a Disability During a Pandemic," *The New York Times*, September 25, 2020, at https://www.nytimes.com/2020/09/25/us/politics/voting-disability-virus.html.

[37] For additional discussion on registration, see CRS Report R46406, *Voter Registration: Recent Developments and Issues for Congress*; and CRS Report R45030, *Federal Role in Voter Registration: The National Voter Registration Act of 1993 and Subsequent Developments*. For additional discussion of signature verification, see, for example, Joint COVID Working Group; Cybersecurity and Infrastructure Security Agency [CISA], Elections Infrastructure Government Coordinating Council, Sector Coordinating Council, *Signature Verification and Cure Process*, Version 1.0. These and related documents are available on the CISA "#PROTECT2020" website, "Election Security GCC and SCC Resources" section, https://www.cisa.gov/protect2020; Rachel Orey and Emma Jones, "Is Voting by Mail Safe and Reliable? We Asked State and Local Elections Officials," Bipartisan Policy Center, June 12, 2020, at https://bipartisanpolicy.org/blog/is-voting-by-mail-safe-and-reliable-we-asked-state-and-local-elections-officials/; and Williiam Janover and Tom Westphal, "Signature Verification and Mail Ballots: Guaranteeing Access While Preserving Integrity—A Case Study of California's Every Vote Counts Act," *Election Law Journal: Rules, Politics, and Policy*, vol. 19, no. 3 (September 2020), pp. 321-343.

[38] See Joint COVID Working Group; Cybersecurity and Infrastructure Security Agency [CISA], Elections Infrastructure Government Coordinating Council, Sector Coordinating Council, *Signature Verification and Cure Process*, Version 1.0. These and related documents are available on the CISA "#PROTECT2020" website, "Election Security GCC and SCC Resources" section, https://www.cisa.gov/protect2020, pp. 3-5; and National Conference of State Legislatures, *VOPP: Table 15: States That Permit Voters to Correct Signature Discrepancies*, August 28, 2020, at https://www.ncsl.org/research/elections-and-campaigns/vopp-table-15-states-that-permit-voters-to-correct-signature-discrepancies.aspx.

[39] National Conference of State Legislatures, *VOPP: Table 14: How States Verify Voted Absentee Ballots*, April 17, 2020, at https://www.ncsl.org/research/elections-and-campaigns/vopp-table-14-how-states-verify-voted-absentee.aspx.

voter.[40] Some states require that a voter return his or her own ballot or limit who, aside from the voter, can return an absentee ballot.[41]

When do states count ballots and certify election results?

The timeline for counting votes can vary, depending on when states and localities allow voters to cast their ballots[42] and when election officials are allowed to begin processing and counting those ballots. The window available for voters to cast ballots varies by state, as jurisdictions have different polling place hours on election day, as well as different policies regarding the availability and duration of in-person early voting and mail voting.[43] In several states, mail ballots are sent, and early in-person voting may begin, at least 45 days ahead of election day.[44] Depending on state law, early voting might end several days before election day or continue until the day before election day. For mail ballots, states vary in whether the ballots must be received on election day or postmarked by election day.[45]

In many states, election officials can begin "processing" absentee ballots they have received before election day, though what "processing" means varies by state. Processing often can involve scanning the tracking barcode on a return ballot envelope and signature verification, where the signature required on the outside of the ballot envelope is compared with a voter's known signature from state registration records. Some states also allow early ballots to be counted before election day, whereas other states prohibit ballots from being counted before polls close on election day.[46] States also vary in how and when they count provisional ballots cast on

---

[40] Darrell M. West, "How does vote-by-mail work and does it increase election fraud," Brookings Institute, June 22, 2020, at https://www.brookings.edu/policy2020/votervital/how-does-vote-by-mail-work-and-does-it-increase-election-fraud/.

[41] National Conference of State Legislatures, *VOPP: Table 10: Who Can Collect and Return an Absentee Ballot Other Than the Voter*, August 28, 2020, at https://www.ncsl.org/research/elections-and-campaigns/vopp-table-10-who-can-collect-and-return-an-absentee-ballot-other-than-the-voter.aspx.

[42] For information on early and mail voting timelines in each state, see National Association of Secretaries of State, *Dates and Deadlines for Early and Absentee Voting in the November 3rd General Election*, August 2020, at https://www.nass.org/node/1967. A list of changes made by states for the 2020 election is available from Ballotpedia, *Changes to election dates, procedures, and administration in response to the coronavirus (COVID-19) pandemic, 2020*, at https://ballotpedia.org/Changes_to_election_dates,_procedures,_and_administration_in_response_to_the_coronavirus_(COVID-19)_pandemic,_2020#Absentee.2Fmail-in_voting_procedure_changes.

[43] The Uniformed and Overseas Citizens Absentee Voting Act (UOCAVA; 52 U.S.C. §§20301-20311) specifies separate requirements for citizens abroad and members of the *uniformed services* (primarily military members). For brief additional discussion, see CRS In Focus IF11642, *Absentee Voting for Uniformed Services and Overseas Citizens: Roles and Process, In Brief*, by R. Sam Garrett.

[44] National Conference of State Legislatures, *State Laws Governing Early Voting*, August 27, 2020, at https://www.ncsl.org/research/elections-and-campaigns/early-voting-in-state-elections.aspx; and National Conference of State Legislatures, *VOPP: Table 7: When States Mail Out Absentee Ballots*, August 24, 2020, at https://www.ncsl.org/research/elections-and-campaigns/vopp-table-7-when-states-mail-out-absentee-ballots.aspx.

[45] National Conference of State Legislatures, *VOPP: Table 11: Receipt and Postmark Deadlines for Absentee Ballots*, September 10, 2020, at https://www.ncsl.org/research/elections-and-campaigns/vopp-table-11-receipt-and-postmark-deadlines-for-absentee-ballots.aspx.

[46] National Conference of State Legislatures, *VOPP Table 16: When Absentee/Mail Ballot Processing and Counting Can Begin*, September 9, 2020, at https://www.ncsl.org/research/elections-and-campaigns/vopp-table-16-when-absentee-mail-ballot-processing-and-counting-can-begin.aspx.

election day.[47] Some states begin counting provisional ballots immediately after polls close, with statutory deadlines ranging from two days to weeks after an election, whereas other states examine provisional ballots as part of the canvass process.[48] Some states do not specify a deadline for their certified election results, and other states have deadlines ranging from November 5 to December 11 for the 2020 general election.[49]

How might the COVID-19 pandemic affect vote count procedures and timing in 2020?

States' actions to expand access to mail voting and voters' concerns about the safety of in-person voting have prompted an increase in mail ballot requests in many states in 2020.[50] Mail ballots require more processing than ballots cast in person and may arrive after the close of polls in jurisdictions that accept ballots postmarked by election day.[51] Unfamiliarity with 2020 mail voting timeframes or procedures—due to general lack of experience with mail voting or changes in processes in response to the COVID-19 pandemic—could lead some voters to make mistakes when completing or submitting mail ballots.[52] Delays, or concerns about delays, in postal service could prompt voters who have requested mail ballots to nevertheless go to the polls in person to vote.[53]

Any or all of those factors could affect vote count procedures and timing in 2020. Voter errors on mail ballots could increase processing time in jurisdictions that offer voters opportunities to cure their ballots, for example, or prompt litigation that delays the release of official results.[54]

---

[47] *Provisional ballot* is a general term used to describe a ballot provided to a voter when there is uncertainty surrounding the voter's eligibility, under circumstances described in HAVA or state law.

[48] National Conference of State Legislatures, *Provisional Ballots*, September 17, 2020, at https://www.ncsl.org/research/elections-and-campaigns/provisional-ballots.aspx; Ballotpedia, *State by State Provisional Ballot Laws*, at https://ballotpedia.org/State_by_State_Provisional_Ballot_Laws.

[49] Ballotpedia, *Election Results Certification Dates, 2020,* at https://ballotpedia.org/Election_results_certification_dates,_2020; and National Association of Secretaries of State, *State Election Canvassing Timeframes and Recount Thresholds*, August 2020, at http://www.nass.org/sites/default/files/surveys/2020-08/summary-canvass-recount-laws-aug2020.pdf.

[50] Adam Levy, Ethan Cohen, and Liz Stark, "Surge of Ballot Requests Already Setting Records in the US," CNN, September 25, 2020, https://www.cnn.com/2020/09/25/politics/ballot-requests-voting-election-2020/index.html.

[51] For more information about processing of mail ballots, see the "What processes help election officials determine voter eligibility and the validity of ballots cast?" section of this report.

[52] Barry Burden, Robert M. Stein, and Charles Stewart III, "More Voting by Mail Would Make the 2020 Election Safer for Our Health. But It Comes with Risks of Its Own.," *The Washington Post*, April 6, 2020, https://www.washingtonpost.com/politics/2020/04/06/more-voting-by-mail-would-make-2020-election-safer-our-health-it-comes-with-risks-its-own/; and National Conference of State Legislatures, *Absentee and Mail Voting Policies in Effect for the 2020 Election*, https://www.ncsl.org/research/elections-and-campaigns/absentee-and-mail-voting-policies-in-effect-for-the-2020-election.aspx.

[53] See, for example, Larry Seward, "With Some Absentee Ballots Still Not Delivered, Indiana Clerk Blames Post Office for Delays," WCPO-ABC Cincinnati, October 1, 2020, at https://www.wcpo.com/news/election-2020/with-some-absentee-ballots-still-not-delivered-indiana-clerk-blames-post-office-for-delays; and Ellie Rushing and Jonathan Lai, "Philly Mail Delays Lead to Big Worries About 2020 Election as Post Office Slows," *The Philadelphia Inquirer*, August 6, 2020, at https://www.inquirer.com/politics/election/mail-voting-phiadelphia-post-office-delays-20200806.html.

[54] Specific information about litigation is beyond the scope of this report. For more information about current COVID-19-related election litigation, see, for example, Stanford-MIT Healthy Elections Project, *COVID-Related Election Litigation Tracker*, https://healthyelections-case-tracker.stanford.edu/search.

Jurisdictions might require in-person voters to use a provisional ballot, which requires additional processing to confirm voter eligibility and prevent double voting, if they are on record as requesting a mail ballot.[55] Depending on how jurisdictions choose to conduct their counts—whether they increase postelection staffing, for example, or extend the timeframe for processing mail ballots—such factors could lead to later release of official election results in some states in 2020 than in previous years.[56]

The COVID-19 pandemic might also affect the 2020 vote count in other ways, in addition to direct and indirect effects of increased mail voting. Increased interest in and expanded access to in-person early voting could help offset effects like those described above, while other results of the pandemic might contribute to them. Health or economic effects of the pandemic could contribute to understaffing of election offices or ballot-processing teams, for example, and COVID-19-related closures or backlogs at offices that process voter registration information could contribute to an increase in provisional voting in some jurisdictions.[57] New or ongoing lawsuits about aspects of the election other than mail voting could also affect the procedures election officials use to tally the 2020 vote and the timeline on which they finalize the count.[58]

How have states responded to potential effects of COVID-19 on the 2020 vote count?

States have responded to some potential effects of the COVID-19 pandemic by trying to minimize or prevent delays in the count and release of official election results. Measures employed by some states include moving up the date when election workers can start processing mail ballots and hiring additional temporary staff to help with ballot processing.[59] Election officials in many jurisdictions are working with local postmasters and United States Postal Service election mail coordinators to help identify ways to facilitate timely delivery of mail ballots, such as by creating color-coded mail ballot return envelopes and providing estimated

---

[55] Edward B. Foley, "Vote Early and Often? That'll Just Slow Down the Ballot Count," *The Washington Post*, September 4, 2020, https://www.washingtonpost.com/outlook/2020/09/04/trump-vote-twice-states/.

[56] See, for example, Jeffrey Toobin, "The Legal Fight Awaiting Us After the Election," *The New Yorker*, September 21, 2020, https://www.newyorker.com/magazine/2020/09/28/the-legal-fight-awaiting-us-after-the-election; and Edward B. Foley, "Why Vote-by-Mail Could Be a Legal Nightmare in November," *Politico*, April 7, 2020, https://www.politico.com/news/magazine/2020/04/07/danger-moving-vote-by-mail-168602.

[57] See, for example, Amy Hudak, "Short Staffing at DMV Due to COVID-19 Creating Voter Registration Backlog," WPXI, October 1, 2020, https://www.wpxi.com/news/short-staffing-dmv-due-covid-19-creating-voter-registration-backlog/K62CCH6UINC7JKYTXJQQLUAVEY/.

[58] Specific information about litigation is beyond the scope of this report. For more information about current COVID-19-related election litigation, see, for example, Stanford-MIT Healthy Elections Project, *COVID-Related Election Litigation Tracker*, https://healthyelections-case-tracker.stanford.edu/search.

[59] Some federal funding made available to states for certain election expenses may be used for these purposes. Congress provided $400 million in the Coronavirus Aid, Relief, and Economic Security (CARES) Act (P.L. 116-136) for grant funding to help states, territories, and the District of Columbia to prevent, prepare for, and respond to COVID-19 under the Help America Vote Act of 2002 (52 U.S.C. §§20901-21145). Congress also provided $425 million to states, territories, and Washington, DC, for general election grant funding in the Consolidated Appropriations Act, 2020 (P.L. 116-93). For more information, see CRS Insight IN11508, *Elections Grant Funding for States: Recent Appropriations and Legislative Proposals*, by Karen L. Shanton. See also, for example, Associated Press, "Michigan Legislature Eases Processing of Absentee Ballots," September 25, 2020, https://www.wxyz.com/news/election-2020/michigan-legislature-eases-processing-of-absentee-ballots; and Brian X. McCrone, "Here's How Pa. Will Get All the Mail-In Ballots Counted in November," NBC Philadelphia, August 31, 2020, https://www.nbcphiladelphia.com/news/politics/decision-2020/heres-how-pa-is-preparing-for-the-presidential-election-in-november/2515837/.

drop-off dates for election mail.[60] Many election officials are also encouraging voters to cast their ballots early, where possible, by returning mail ballots promptly or taking advantage of in-person early voting periods.[61]

In addition to trying to minimize or prevent delays in the release of official election results, many jurisdictions have taken steps to educate voters about the potential for and meaning of any delays that do occur. A concern some have raised about the 2020 elections is that delays in the release of official results might lead some to question the legitimacy of the election.[62] Many states have responded to such concerns by sharing public information about typical postelection processes and timelines or adapting their plans for initial results reporting to more clearly convey the incompleteness of unofficial results. In one state, for example, the secretary of state announced that early reporting would include data on the number of requested mail ballots that had not yet been counted to provide a sense of the potential scope of outstanding ballots.[63]

What processes are available if disputes remain after election results are certified?

Different terminology applies to various scenarios surrounding disputed election results. The term *recount* refers to retabulating ballots to ensure that the certified count was accurate (although, in some jurisdictions, recounts might occur before certification).[64] Election officials generally conduct recounts when elections result in very close margins of victory to confirm that the certified results are accurate, or if there is evidence that counting equipment malfunctioned.[65] There are two kinds of recounts: automatic and requested. Typically, a narrow margin of victory

---

[60] United States Postal Service Office of Inspector General, *Audit Report: Processing Readiness of Mail During the 2020 General Election*, August 31, 2020, pp. 3-4, https://www.uspsoig.gov/sites/default/files/document-library-files/2020/20-225-R20.pdf. Some concerns have been raised in the lead-up to the 2020 elections about potential effects of operational changes at the United States Postal Service on delivery of mail ballots. For additional discussion of such concerns, see U.S. Congress, Senate Committee on Homeland Security and Governmental Affairs, *Examining the Finances and Operations of the United States Postal Service During COVID-19 and Upcoming Elections*, hearing, 116th Cong., 2nd sess., August 21, 2020, https://www.hsgac.senate.gov/examining-the-finances-and-operations-of-the-united-states-postal-service-during-covid-19-and-upcoming-elections; and U.S. Congress, House Committee on Oversight and Reform, *Protecting the Timely Delivery of Mail, Medicine, and Mail-in Ballots*, hearing, 116th Cong., 2nd sess., August 24, 2020, https://oversight.house.gov/legislation/hearings/protecting-the-timely-delivery-of-mail-medicine-and-mail-in-ballots.

[61] See, for example, Star Connor, "WV Secretary of State Encourages Absentee Ballot Voting," WVVA, September 24, 2020, https://wvva.com/2020/09/24/wv-secretary-of-state-encourages-absentee-ballot-voting/; and Blake Keller and Brianna Owczarzak, "Whitmer Encourages Residents to Vote as Early Voting Kicks Off Across Michigan," WNEM, September 24, 2020, https://www.wnem.com/news/whitmer-encourages-residents-to-vote-as-early-voting-kicks-off-across-michigan/article_e38d9e62-fe70-11ea-9282-a7359f85ceef.html.

[62] See, for example, Andy Sullivan and Michael Martina, "How a 'Blue Shift' in U.S. Mail Ballots Might Set Off Election Week Chaos," Reuters, September 8, 2020, https://www.reuters.com/article/us-usa-election-delay/how-a-blue-shift-in-u-s-mail-ballots-might-set-off-election-week-chaos-idUSKBN25Z1I1.

[63] Andrew J. Tobias, "Preparing for Possibly Unclear Result, Ohio Will Report the Number of Outstanding Mail Ballots on Election Night," *Cleveland.com*, September 8, 2020, https://www.cleveland.com/open/2020/09/preparing-for-possibly-unclear-result-ohio-will-report-the-number-of-outstanding-mail-ballots-on-election-night.html.

[64] For example, the U.S. Election Assistance Commission Voluntary Voting System Guidelines define *recount* as "[r]etabulation of the votes cast in an election." See U.S. Election Assistance Commission, *Voluntary Voting System Guidelines*, Vol. 1, Version 1.1 (2015), p. A-16.

[65] See, for example, U.S. Election Assistance Commission, *Election Management Guidelines*, p. 147. The *Election Management Guidelines* document is available on the EAC website at https://www.eac.gov/election_management_resources/election_management_guidelines.aspx.

in an individual race (e.g., less than one-half percent in some states) triggers an *automatic recount* as specified in state statutes. In other cases, candidates or voters may *request* recounts (sometimes called *initiated* recounts), often at their expense and under processes specified in state statutes.[66] Relevant state, territorial, or local election statutes specify which recount options are available in particular jurisdictions, if any, and under what circumstances.

States or other election jurisdictions conduct recounts either by rescanning ballots or by hand counting, depending on circumstances and relevant requirements, and may address all or part of the certified results. Recounts also may involve a *recanvass*—in some states a separate process— to reexamine the validity of the ballots included in the certified results. Election officials, recount boards, or both typically conduct recounts.

Although timing varies by state, statutes typically limit the period during which recounts may occur. Election officials can face particularly tight deadlines for conducting recounts if they occur shortly before officeholders-elect are to be sworn in. In addition, for presidential elections, a federal "safe harbor" deadline may affect how long states have to conduct their recounts in presidential elections.[67]

Election *contests* focus on the circumstances surrounding the conduct of the election. As with recounts, contests follow processes addressed in relevant state law. Generally, contests are resolved through litigation that is beyond the scope of this report. The Federal Contested Election Act (FCEA) provides procedures for resolving contested U.S. House elections.[68] Ultimately, Article I, Section 5 of the U.S. Constitution specifies that each chamber of Congress "shall be the Judge of the Elections, Returns and Qualifications of its own Members." Other CRS products provide information on related topics concerning contested U.S. House elections,[69] the electoral college,[70] and the congressional role in verifying and counting presidential election results.[71]

---

[66] For example, as the National Conference of State Legislatures (NCSL) has explained, "although post-election audits can lead to a full recount if errors are detected, they differ from a recount in that they are conducted regardless of the margins of victory. Recounts are most often triggered or requested if there is a tight margin of victory." See National Conference of State Legislatures, "Post-Election Audits," October 25, 2019, https://www.ncsl.org/research/elections-and-campaigns/post-election-audits635926066.aspx.

[67] For additional discussion, see CRS In Focus IF11641, *The Electoral College: A 2020 Presidential Election Timeline*, by Thomas H. Neale; and CRS Report R40504, *Contingent Election of the President and Vice President by Congress: Perspectives and Contemporary Analysis*, by Thomas H. Neale.

[68] 2 U.S.C. §§381-396. For additional discussion, see CRS Report RL33780, *Procedures for Contested Election Cases in the House of Representatives*, by L. Paige Whitaker.

[69] See CRS Report RL33780, *Procedures for Contested Election Cases in the House of Representatives*, by L. Paige Whitaker.

[70] See, for example, CRS In Focus IF11641, *The Electoral College: A 2020 Presidential Election Timeline*, by Thomas H. Neale; CRS Report R43824, *Electoral College Reform: Contemporary Issues for Congress*, by Thomas H. Neale; and CRS Report R40504, *Contingent Election of the President and Vice President by Congress: Perspectives and Contemporary Analysis*, by Thomas H. Neale.

[71] See CRS Report RL32717, *Counting Electoral Votes: An Overview of Procedures at the Joint Session, Including Objections by Members of Congress*, coordinated by Elizabeth Rybicki and L. Paige Whitaker.

Supreme Court Clarifies Rules for Electoral College: States May Restrict Faithless Electors

July 10, 2020   LSB10515

On July 6, 2020, the Supreme Court unanimously held that states may punish or replace presidential electors who refuse to cast their ballots for the candidate chosen by the voters of their state. In the case *Chiafalo v. Washington*, a majority of the Court held that the State of Washington's constitutional authority to appoint electors includes the power to impose a $1,000 fine against electors who violate their pledge to support the candidate chosen in the state's popular vote. In the related case *Colorado Department of State v. Baca*, the Court upheld on the same grounds Colorado's policy of replacing electors who attempt to cast a ballot for a person who did not win the state's popular vote. This Legal Sidebar explains the Court's decisions and reviews their broader implications.

Background

Article II of the Constitution provides, "Each State shall appoint, in such Manner as the Legislature thereof may direct, a Number of Electors, equal to the whole Number of Senators and Representatives to which the State may be entitled in the Congress." Under the Twelfth Amendment, the electors "meet in their respective states and vote by ballot for President and Vice-President, one of whom, at least, shall not be an inhabitant of the same state with themselves."

Today, states employ a two-step process to appoint their electors. First, states ask each political party to submit a slate of electors that it would like to represent the state. Second, states hold a general election in November—what is widely regarded as Election Day—where voters register their preference among candidates for President and Vice President. The party that wins the most statewide votes for its presidential ticket generally gets to have its slate of electors appointed by the state. (Forty-eight states and the District of Columbia allot all their electoral votes to the winner of the statewide popular vote; Maine and Nebraska allot two electors to the winner of the statewide popular vote and one elector to the winner of the popular vote in each of the state's congressional districts.)

Because political parties choose the electors in the first instance, electors are expected to be loyal to their party and cast ballots for the party's ticket if its candidates win the state vote. But that expectation has not always come true. Occasionally, so-called "faithless electors" cast ballots for candidates other than those their parties prefer—sometimes as a form of political protest, sometimes as a strategic ploy, and sometimes, apparently, by mistake. To curb these surprises, 32 states and the District of Columbia have enacted laws requiring electors to pledge to cast their votes for their parties' nominees for President and Vice President, with 15 states providing some form of sanction for electors who violate their pledge. The Supreme Court upheld the constitutionality of these pledge requirements in the 1952 case *Ray v. Blair* but had not yet weighed in on whether states may enforce the requirements with sanctions.

Washington and Colorado provide two representative illustrations of how some states seek to ensure that electors cast ballots for candidates supported by the states' voters. Washington requires prospective electors to pledge to support their party's candidates and, in 2016, subjected electors who violated their pledge to a $1,000 fine. This punishment was imposed on Brian Chiafalo and two other Democratic electors who were appointed after Hillary Clinton won the state's popular vote but who chose instead to cast their ballots for Colin Powell. The electors challenged the fines as unconstitutional, arguing that states are powerless to restrict an elector's exercise of discretion. The Washington Supreme Court disagreed, reasoning that nothing in the Constitution demands absolute freedom of choice for electors, and upheld the punishment.

Colorado, in turn, discards the ballot of any elector who fails to vote for the presidential ticket that won the most votes in the state's popular election, replacing rogue electors with alternates until all electors have submitted ballots for the ticket that received the most votes on Election Day. Democratic elector Michael Baca suffered this fate in 2016 after attempting to cast his ballot for John Kasich; his vote was nullified, and he was removed from his position as elector. Like the Washington electors, he challenged his state's law as an unconstitutional interference with what he viewed as a discretionary vote. But unlike the Washington court, the Tenth Circuit ruled in favor of elector discretion and struck down Colorado's law on the grounds that electors have a constitutional right to vote for whomever they wish. The Supreme Court agreed to hear appeals from these two cases to settle the issue.

Supreme Court Decision

In *Chiafalo v. Washington*, the Supreme Court unanimously held that states may penalize electors who fail to cast their ballots for the presidential ticket that won the state's popular vote. Justice Kagan authored a majority opinion joined by Chief Justice Roberts and Justices Ginsburg, Breyer, Alito, Sotomayor, Gorsuch, and Kavanaugh, holding that state authority under Article II to appoint electors includes the power to require as a condition of appointment that electors pledge to support the state's popular vote winner and—as relevant here—to punish electors who violate that pledge. Justice Thomas authored an opinion concurring in the judgment, joined in part by Justice Gorsuch, arguing that states' power to prohibit faithless electors is more appropriately rooted in the Tenth Amendment. In *Colorado Department of State v. Baca*, the Court published a one-sentence, per curiam order reversing the Tenth Circuit for the reasons explained by the majority in *Chiafalo*. Justice Sotomayor was recused from *Baca* because of her friendship with one of the parties.

The majority opinion in *Chiafalo* read Article II of the Constitution to provide states with a broad power to appoint electors and determined that any limits on that power could be derived only from some other constitutional provision. Reviewing the Constitution's "barebones" text about the Electoral College process, the Court concluded that neither Article II nor any other part of the Constitution limited a state's ability to require electors to cast their ballots for the candidate that won the state's popular vote. According to Justice Kagan, Article II empowers states to appoint electors, and the Twelfth Amendment provides simple procedures for how the electors' ballots are to be submitted and counted. "Appointments and procedures," the Court summarized, "and … that is all." The Court reasoned that if the Constitution's drafters intended to secure electors' prerogative to vote according to their own judgment, as some including Alexander Hamilton seem to have hoped, they could have adopted language from contemporary state constitutions that included explicit safeguards for the autonomy of electoral bodies that selected state officials. But the Court concluded the Twelfth Amendment's terse instruction that electors shall "vote by ballot" imposes no such requirement of elector independence.

The Court emphasized that the Twelfth Amendment was necessary, at least in part, to facilitate electors' practice of party-line voting. Before the Amendment was ratified in 1804, each elector cast two votes, with no distinction made between electoral votes for President and electoral votes for Vice President. The candidate receiving a majority of votes became President and the runner-up became Vice President. The problem, which soon became apparent, was that if electors for the most popular party submitted their two ballots for the party's candidates for President and Vice President, those candidates would tie and no one would receive the requisite majority—as occurred in 1800 (and, as the Court recognized, was later immortalized in the Broadway hit *Hamilton*). Alternatively, if those electors intentionally cast fewer votes for the intended Vice President, they risked allowing another party's presidential candidate to sneak into the top two. This was no hypothetical fear—the 1796 election resulted in a President and Vice President from rival parties. "By allowing the electors to vote separately for the two offices," the *Chiafalo* Court concluded, "the Twelfth Amendment made party-line voting safe." An Amendment ratified to accommodate party-line voting, the Court reasoned, should not be interpreted to prevent electors from binding themselves with declarations of party loyalty.

Noting that historical practice can help settle the meaning of disputed constitutional terms, the Court determined that "[e]lectors have only rarely exercised discretion in casting their ballots for President." According to the Court's tally, only one half of 1 percent of all electoral votes in American history have been for a person other than the candidate who won the popular vote in the elector's home state, and these anomalous votes have never come close to affecting an outcome. Electors have been declaring their loyalty to their party's candidates since the nation's first contested election in 1796, and by the early 1900s states began requiring prospective electors to execute such a pledge as a condition of appointment. Washington's law, the Court concluded, "reflects a tradition more than two centuries old. In that practice, electors are not free agents; they are to vote for the candidate whom the State's voters have chosen."

The Court cautioned that states' power under Article II to condition the appointment of electors, while broad, is not limitless. For example, a state may not select its electors in a manner that violates the Equal Protection Clause, and a state may not restrict which candidates electors may vote for in a way that conflicts with the Presidential Qualifications Clause (perhaps, for example, by requiring electors to pledge to vote only for candidates who possess previous government experience). Further, the Court explicitly refrained from deciding whether a state could enforce its pledge requirements if the state's popular vote winner died between Election Day and the date that electors submit their ballots.

In a separate opinion concurring in the judgment, Justice Thomas agreed with the majority that states have the power to require presidential electors to vote for the candidate chosen by their state. But in his view, that power is not derived from Article II or any other Electoral College provision of the Constitution. Rather, he would resolve the case under the Tenth Amendment, which provides, "The powers not delegated to the United States by the Constitution, nor prohibited by it to the States, are reserved to the States respectively, or to the people." Because the Constitution does not explicitly prohibit states from enacting laws that punish or remove faithless electors, he would hold those laws are a valid exercise of state power. Justice Gorsuch joined the majority opinion and the portion of Justice Thomas's concurrence urging that constitutional silence should be resolved in the states' favor, suggesting his view is that the state laws could be upheld both on Article II and Tenth Amendment grounds.

Implications for Congress

The Twelfth Amendment assigns Congress the role of counting the votes submitted by electors and declaring a winner. Historically, Congress's counting role has included the task of resolving controversies when a state's electoral votes are disputed. By statute, Members of Congress may object to individual electoral votes or to state returns as a whole, and the objections are resolved by separate votes in the House and Senate. Because the Supreme Court affirmed states' right to replace faithless electors, and Congress defers to states to decide in the first instance "any controversy or contest concerning the appointment of" electors, the Court's decision may reduce the likelihood that faithless elector disputes will fall to Congress. But the potential for controversy persists in states that require electors to vote for the state's popular vote winner but fail to attach any consequences for electors who vote for someone else. In such a scenario, Members of Congress may need to decide internally whether to count the anomalous votes.

In the event that electors fail to agree on a President and Vice President by majority vote, the Twelfth Amendment provides that the House of Representative shall choose the President and the Senate shall choose the Vice President. Faithless electors have never deprived a presidential candidate of an electoral majority, and by permitting states to punish or replace electors who vote independently, the Supreme Court's decision makes it even less likely that faithless electors will splinter the vote and throw the election to the House and Senate.

The Supreme Court recognized that permitting states to bind electors to the state's popular vote winner accords with "the trust of a Nation that here, We the People rule." That democratic presumption notwithstanding, the Electoral College does limit popular rule by enabling a candidate to win the vote in enough individual states to accumulate an Electoral College majority despite failing to win the most votes nationally. To prevent this discrepancy, some Members of Congress have proposed amending the Constitution to abolish the Electoral College. As another means to a similar end, 15 states and the District of Columbia have enacted laws under the National Popular Vote initiative that would appoint electors pledged to the party that wins the national popular vote rather than to the party that wins the state's popular vote. (These laws would take effect only if they are enacted by enough states that collectively control a majority of the 538 electoral votes; currently, the scheme needs the support of states with an additional 74 electoral votes.) By affirming that Article II allows each state to appoint electors "in whatever way it likes," the Supreme Court's opinion in *Chiafalo* could be read to suggest the plan, if enacted, would survive constitutional challenge.

Printed in Great Britain
by Amazon